Sex Is For Love

Based on the life of a Bipolar II, Lesbian, Sex Addict

Jules Alexander

chipmunkapublishing
the mental health publisher

Published by
Chipmunkapublishing
United Kingdom

http://www.chipmunkapublishing.com

Copyright © 2015 Jules Alexander

ISBN   978-1-78382-146-4

Chipmunkapublishing gratefully acknowledge the support of Arts Council England.

Chapter 1
Understanding the Beginning

In life it seems like we have a handful of decisions that will affect the rest of our lives. I had one recently: to go or not to go. Doesn't that sound so trivial? It does, right? That, my friend, is what makes or breaks most things in our lives.

Some "to go or not to go" decisions are about money, love, integrity, faith, self-preservation. But this "to go or not to go" was pure ego. How dare this middle-aged goalie on this torn indoor soccer field try and stop me from my goal. Doesn't she know me? I will hurt her or any human that gets in the way of my goals, and in this situation it was definitely just one goal. I ran toward the goalie, trying to get there before she did. Then I realized that I made the wrong decision. She would get to the ball before me, so I jumped in the air to try and get out of her way. I didn't make it and in the air everyone heard a "POP".

As I landed on the ground thoughts began running through my head. "Oh, fucking son of a bitch, I only have $5000.00 in savings. This is bad really bad; did anyone call an ambulance? I can work with a broken leg; I'll be out in one or two weeks. Fuck, I have too many babies; I'm going to get up." These were some of the thoughts that went through my head but what came out was so raw and real; strange how times of crisis bring out ones true self. I yelled, "Someone call an ambulance, I'm broken!" How right I was, broken in so many ways, way beyond a broken tibia.

The ambulance came and they lifted me into the back.

"Do you want me to start an IV so that I can give you some pai..."

I didn't let her get the whole sentence out before I said, "yes, yes." It didn't help enough and I tried not to cry too much. I didn't want to look like a baby. Seems like I'm always trying to not appear what I actually am or what I'm actually feeling. I've become a master of disguise, and it has only been during the last couple of years that I have begun to trust myself with my emotions.

Twenty years earlier I was sitting on the couch when my Dad walked through the door with a puppy in his hands. He knew that I wasn't happy and he chalked it up to me being a teenager. I guess he thought the puppy would snap me out of it. It never entered his mind that it might have something to do with him being an abusive alcoholic or the fact that my mother abandoned me for meth and men. Or was it men first and meth second? Who knows? I believed the only reason I felt hollow and had the complete inability to find any light or happiness had to do with that very fact. Little did I know that it would be 20 years from that day that I would know the real reason for what I was feeling, what I was not able to control and what I was not able to shake.

When I was four I begged my parents to play soccer; I was much like my baby son. "I want a coach, Ma, I want a coach..." "Okay coach, what you want me to do, coach?" I felt the same way; I wanted to compete to show the others that I was superior, faster, stronger and better. It wasn't long until I was the one all coaches tried to get on their teams.

I had issues at home so I had to be picked up most of the time for practices and games. I had to be the best because I knew if I wasn't the best I could not be saved for those glorious short hours that I had on the soccer field or softball field. If I wasn't the best, no one would pick me up, right? If I was bad, I thought I wouldn't get to play either, and not playing meant that I was worthless and not worth breathing air. So I worked harder, played harder and tried harder than all the other girls. Sports and competing was the only way I felt worth anything. When I scored a goal or caught a ball it allowed me to feel good for a moment. I became a goal addict; it was my drug. But it wore off soon, as drugs do, and it left me searching for the next high like a drug addict on the street. I was to be the best at everything because in my mind, not winning was not an option. "You will win at everything, Jules." Winning was the only way I felt anything good, anything good had to coming from winning and I beat people at any cost. I would tackle, spit, intimidate, practice longer, play harder – anything to win, winning was the only option. Because of this I didn't have too many friends growing up. My only friend was my big sister.

So let's go to the beginning. I was born to David and Jean Alexander in Atlanta, Georgia. My mom was nervous that I was not going to be healthy because my dad kicked her in the stomach when she was five months pregnant, but I must have dodged that kick like so many other times to come. I had a big sister: Jennifer Alexander, a gorgeous tan- skinned brunette with big hazel eyes. She was my everything for so much of my life; I have to say she still is in so many ways. My father worked for my great-grandfather, David Scott Alexander, the founder of an extremely successful Miami business. He was a brilliant "business man" as many would say, but an alcoholic like his son and his son's son, a disease no one seems to get away from in the Alexander family.

David Scott started another company in Atlanta and my father was helping him run it, but soon Dad got homesick for his native Miami and we moved back within a year.

My early years I cannot remember. I only begin to remember when I was seven, but I do remember one thing: My mother and father were getting ready to go out and I was devastated, and my mother thought that it was because they were leaving me. It wasn't. I was devastated because I knew that it would end up with Mommy and Daddy fighting, really fighting. My dad would call my mom a slut and smack her, and my mother would fight back as much as she could. My dad was 6'3 and 250 pounds and my mom was 5'7 and 120 pounds, so not much of a fair fight. My dad didn't care, he would beat the shit out of her and she would yell back in her Drunken stupor and I would cry and yell, "Daddy leave her alone, Daddy leave her alone. Mommy stop screaming!"

My sister and I would huddle in the corner together until it was done and it would end with my Mom picking us up, smelling of booze and cigarettes and we would to the "Motel". The "Motel" was our place of solitude, a place where my mom would sober up and buy us Taco Bell on the corner of 4th and Green and Jennifer and I would stop crying because we knew that our mother was not strong enough to take it. My mom was not strong enough to hear us cry. In a day or two we would go from the motel to school and when school ended my mom and dad would pick us up like nothing ever happened. Was I crazy? All I knew was that my parents weren't drunk, stoned or fighting, so I felt safe for a little while.

I walked into our home on Pebble Place in Miami Florida and my mother sat us down on the couch. "I have something to tell you girls." Jennifer and I looked at each other and we knew what she was going to say. "Your father and I are getting a divorce. No more fighting, isn't that good news?" I looked at my mom and I could see in her eyes that she was relieved and happy. I knew at an early age that my mom was such a weak woman and even at seven I realized that I needed to react in a way that would allow my mother to feel good. Even though my sister and I didn't speak of this until we were older, it was an unspoken rule when we were younger. React the right way so that Mom would be okay!

"Are you happy Mommy?"

"Yes, Jules. No more fighting, won't that be great?"

"Yes, Mommy. I'm so happy!" Jennifer and I jumped on the couches yelling screams of happiness for my mother. Inside I wondered how my dad was, where he was and if he was okay.

My dad struggled in so many ways; his mind did not let him rest. This was something that I didn't realize I would have to battle through my life as well, having a mind that would not let you rest. He was tormented with anger and heartache from his childhood. But he was a good man underneath all of this. He loved us and we never questioned that.

Jennifer and I knew that we had a "Good Dad" and a "Bad Dad". When the Bad Dad was out you had to walk on eggshells and do everything you could not to send him into a rage. When the Good Dad was out, he was so good, he was the best. He played catch with me, cuddled me, fixed all of my hurts with kisses and hugs. He was a good man, but a tormented man.

Every Wednesday my father would pick us up to go to the Sizzler. He was never late and I was always excited to see my dad. We were so similar; we were both athletes, so I felt a special connection to him. He had a 1979 silver Ford F150 and Jennifer would make me sit in the middle and we would drive to the Sizzler. We would talk about our days since we had seen him and I would tell him over and over again that I loved him, and he would tell me that he loved me too. "I love you too, little one," he would say. Sometimes he would let my sister drive on his lap in the parking lot and I would yell and scream that she was going to crash and kill us and Jennifer would always tell me to "chill out, sis." Chilling out has never come to me naturally, but I knew that my father would not let us crash. Strange feelings I had for my father. I knew that he was not going let anything bad happen to us, but on the other hand I was so frightened of the Bad Dad. Two dads, one body.

Most of the time we had such a great dinner, but sometimes the Bad Dad would come out. You never knew what was going to trigger him. "God dammit Jules, eat the fucking baked potato and stop trying to make it perfect. You remind me of your fucking mother, you spoiled little fuck brat. Eat it now, you fucking little piece of shit, NOW!" Heads would turn in the restaurant, but no one challenged him. My dad was a big man and he looked intimidating, so I understood that it was up to me and Jennifer to calm him down. "Okay Dad, I'm sorry Dad, I won't fuss with the potato." Jennifer and I would put our heads down and eat our dinner and my mind would be spinning on how to make him calm down. "Dad, I scored two goals last weekend!" He would acknowledge, but it was too soon, so I shut my mouth and finished eating. He dropped us off without a word said, but I would tell him that I loved him anyway as he sped off.

The next day my Good Dad would call. "Hi little one, I was thinking about you. I love you. What do you want to do this weekend?" Every other weekend my father would pick us up and we would stay with him. Jennifer soon found friends at the apartment complex and that meant that they would have to play with me too. She would tell all her friends, "You better be nice to my little sister," and they would. Jennifer was good at making me feel like they liked me too. Everyone wanted to be around Jennifer, so if you wanted to be Jennifer's friend you better be nice to the pushy, bossy little sister Jules.

Not having friends was my own fault; I was mean, bossy and fiercely competitive. My parents were so busy trying to survive in their lost and trapped minds; they were unable to parent me and teach me how to get along with others. Jennifer on the other hand had such a bright glow that if you knew her you wanted to be around her, period. This is something that she still has to this day and it's amazing to watch.

My dad's apartment was just like those of most single men in their early thirties with kids: two bedrooms and a living room filled with workout equipment. He placed my trophies on a mantel and always told me how proud he was of me. "Natural athlete Jules, that's what you are, little one." I wondered what he did when we were not there. What did he do, and whom did he see? Was he sad, as sad as I was that he was not living with us?

My father's sadness was beyond missing us, though it was apparent if you looked in his eyes that he struggled with every smile and with anger with everything good in life. My father was such a vicious and kind man. Those two words usually don't go together, but they did when you described my father.

I was on the soccer field and I knew it was getting close to 6pm. Practice was supposed to be over and I knew there would be hell to pay if I was not in the parking lot at 5:59pm. My father was struggling with his anger that day. I could tell because he didn't talk much when he dropped me off. When he didn't talk much it meant that he was fighting the Bad Dad. At five past six I asked my coach to leave. He said that we were almost finished. I knew I was in trouble. My mind was racing. How was I going to leave without everyone thinking I was stupid, or weird?

My father appeared. "Jules. Jules! Get in the fucking truck!" He was on the field yelling my name in front of my coaches and teammates. At this point I wasn't worried about appearing stupid in front of everyone. I just went into survival mode, as my sister and I often did. "Okay Dad." One of my coaches took a step toward me. I wanted him to go away because I knew my dad would hurt him if he tried to defend me. "David, we are almost done," the coach said. My dad replied, "You said the practice was until six. It's now ten past six and if you want Jules on this team you will make sure she is in the parking lot at 5:59pm. Do I make myself clear?" Remember, my dad was 6'3 and 250 pounds he was a big man and he was intimidating to the strongest men. "Okay David," was all the coach said. My father grabbed my shirt and led me off the field.

When we were out of sight of the others he grabbed my ponytail and yanked me to the ground. "You fucking little spoiled brat. Who do you think you are?" I knew the torment was going to last a while this time. He was not trying to fight it anymore. He had surrendered to the Bad Dad, and when this happened the Bad Dad would be out until he drank enough and smoked enough pot to pass out. "Jules, you are a piece of shit! Do you hear me you little fucking bitch?" We were driving home and I had my head down so my father new I was submitting to his anger, hoping it would make the night a bit better. The back of my head began to hurt now where he had yanked me to the ground and I tried not to cry. Crying would make Bad Dad even more angry, and this amount of anger was enough tonight. "You think you are hot shit because people want you on their teams, well let me tell you different. If you want to play soccer, if you want me to run around like a bitch for you, you will respect my time. Do you understand me?" I turned to look at my father and I could see the Bad Dad. His face was red and his eyes matched. Saliva was forming on the sides of his mouth and when he yelled a piece of spit found a home on my face. I didn't wipe it from my face because I didn't know that would make things worse. If I cried I knew it would start the ranting: "What are you crying for you little bitch, I was the one that had to wait for an undeserving spoiled fucking brat." So I sat and listened to the never-ending rage.

It never changed. It always had "fucking," "bitch" and "spoiled" mixed in with "undeserving". It never changed and that's what made it so hard. I still hear that track to this day; at 37 I'm still effected by this never-ending track in my mind. No matter how much therapy, how much talking – anytime I mess anything up it starts: "You fucking little bitch, you are a piece of shit, you are worth nothing, you are nothing you are a waste of my time!" At 37 and even with both dads dead, the Bad Dad and the Good Dad still live in my head and the Bad Dad usually wins the track rights in my head. At 37, can you believe it?

My father was born to Dick and Melody Alexander. His story is so outrageous it almost doesn't seem real. Dick Alexander, my dad's father, was the son of David Alexander, a rich businessman. Dick never had to worry about anything; he was born with a silver spoon in his mouth. David put him in all the best schools, took him to all the best parties and did all the right things for Dick. Even with all the right things Dick became an alcoholic. Not the "I'm going to have 5-10 drinks a night"-kind like my father who gets up by 7am the next day. He was on the drink for two weeks at a time and would black out in an alley and wake up in the hospital not knowing how he got there. He was a happy drunk but unable to control his life; alcohol controlled him.

One afternoon Dick drove into a truck stop in South Carolina, close to the Blue Ridge Mountains. He was on spring break from college and was driving around with a friend trying to find a good time. He purchased gas and went to the diner with his friend to get a bite to eat. The rest of the story in unknown, but this is what ended up happening: Dick met my grandmother Jean. She was a waitress at the diner. Apparently they hit it off and had a great time – well, that is speculation, but what is not speculation is that Jean ended up pregnant in those two weeks with my Aunt Melody. Dick married

Jean and they had a little baby girl, then a boy, my father, and then finished off the litter with another boy.

Jean, my grandmother, was raised quite differently than my grandfather. Her father was a moonshiner in the Blue Ridge Mountains and she had eleven brothers a sister. They lived in a shack up in the mountains. I met her once when I was eleven, but I don't remember too much. Dick moved Jean to Miami. But she didn't fit in. She was a mountain woman, a big thick mountain woman who did not understand nor care to understand manners. She was taller than my grandfather, and from what my dad says she used to beat the shit out of him on a regular basis. My dad would laugh and say, "I used to have to call the police and say, my mom is beating the shit out of my dad." He said the police never believed him and would say, "Son, do you mean that your dad is beating up your mom?" He laughed when he said it, but I knew even as a kid it hurt him.

My dad's parents would leave for weeks at a time and not leave any money for food for the kids. My dad and his brother and sister would look through the house to find money to get ice cream on the ice cream truck. Could you imagine coming from one of the wealthiest families in Miami at the time and not have enough food to eat? He used to say that they had a huge house with everything money could buy, even a pool in the shape of a K, but he spent a lot of his childhood hungry because his parents would take off for days, if not weeks at a time. Jean used to abuse my father physically and her other kids, too.

I saw Naomi Judd say on her reality show the other day that she is convinced that her family had a curse. I sat up when she explained why and I believed her when she was done. I thought, "My god, we have a curse too." So many brilliant, talented beautiful people in my family, but we always fall short. We all have had so many opportunities for greatness but when that moment comes, the "to do or not to do"-moment, we always fuck it up and make the wrong choice at the crossroad. I've managed to become somewhat successful in sales, but only because I refuse to let my dad win. I refuse to be a piece of shit and/or to give in to the family curse.

Okay, enough on my dad's parents and childhood. To sum it up, here goes: Rich granddad marries huge hillbilly woman, brings her back to the city, huge hillbilly woman kicks the shit out of rich granddad and everyone else. The grandparents have a lot of money from the great- grandpa and do nothing with it but party. Hillbilly leaves rich granddad and moves back to the Blue Ridge Mountains and is never heard from again. You've heard the story, right? Moving on.

So you are probably thinking, what about my mom, right? I know, me too; what kind of fucked up family did she come from to leave her own kids for meth and men? I can't really figure it out myself. My mom's parents were normal, I think. My granddad sold cars and then bought a motorcycle dealership and made good money. My grandma was a beautiful woman—aww, therein lies the problem! Beautiful women are trouble, they really are. Trust me, I know, I'm a lesbian. Oh shit, I lost you. Forget I said that, the lesbian thing, I will get back to that later. Beautiful grandma marries beautiful grandfather: okay, I just figured it out. Everyone in that family was beautiful, even the kids.

My grandmother wanted to be in show business and my grandfather wanted a stay-at-home wife. So his wife stayed home and made her children miserable and the grandfather cheated on her with tons of women. (Hey, another revelation: I mirrored my grandfather in my twenties, because I too slept with lots of married women. Okay, I have it backwards; I wasn't married at the time, the pseudo-straight women were married. Well dammit, in my defense, these pseudo- straight woman didn't seem straight when we were having sex, they really didn't trust me. Oh, fuck it again, forget I said anything.)

Okay, I'm lost. I don't even know if I'm supposed to start another paragraph here, I'm so adrift with what I was trying to say. I'm going to start another paragraph because I think that's what I'm supposed to do.

Back to my mother's childhood. All I know is that every child that came from those two struggled with light in their life. My aunt robbed a jewelry store in her early twenties, and then when she got out of prison she became addicted to heroin. My other aunt was a pretty successful model, but at 27 she thought she was worthless and old, so she signed up for a self-help seminar and it turned out to be a cult. The cult convinced her that she didn't need her asthma inhaler and that if she believed in God enough her asthma attack would go away. She tried to believe what they were saying. She needed something; a Glass without her looks was like, well, a nothing. So she tried to believe and died in the process. My uncle married an extremely dominant woman that told him when to do everything; she took care of him like a child until he in died in his early fifties. Five days ago my mom sent me a mug shot of my aunt (the one that went to prison). She's back on drugs and recently got arrested. She was doing good until her looks started fading, and then she couldn't manipulate men any longer and they wouldn't put up with her shit. So being the weak woman she is, boom, back on drugs.

My mother: sad story, really. As you know she left my sister and me to pursue drugs and men. Both drugs and men were not real good to her, so on her down times she would crawl back to me and

Jennifer and tell us how much she loved us. Months or sometimes days would pass and back to men or drugs, whichever came along first.

As you read the first part of this book you would think that my dad hurt me and my sister the most, but I have to say it's an even-steven as far as I can tell. What woman leaves her kids for drugs and men and leaves them with a man she knows has a huge rage problem? Even today I have a hard time seeing my mother or hearing her voice. She says she's sorry and cries the cries and says how much Jennifer and I and the grandkids mean to her. Jennifer and I secretly believe that if a man came along we would be thrown from the moving car faster than you could say zerbert. Now she just drinks about 6-10 beers a night and this is a huge improvement, so in a very, very, very sad way we are happy for that.

I was nine the day I realized that my childhood was never going to be easy. My mom had just broken up with her divorce attorney (another perk of being beautiful – free legal fees) and she had been drinking all day and night for days. We were still living with her, but it was getting so bad that my dad was starting to worry about us with her.

It was about 3pm; I walked in the door from walking home from school. Jennifer wasn't there yet; she probably got a ride with one of her million friends. I was kind of excited, hoping that my mom was going to be sober and that we could have some time together. I opened the door and saw my mom naked on the couch. She looked like she had been sitting on the couch and fell forward with her head on the ground. I immediately started to cry. I knew something was wrong, I didn't know what but I knew something was really wrong. I ran to her and at that moment my sister walked in. Erin Barlow's mom had dropped Jennifer off and I think I told Jennifer to stop her, I don't really remember. All I knew was that my mom was lifeless and I knew she was dead. I screamed, "Mommy no, Mommy don't die, don't leave me Mommy," over and over.

The next couple of hours and days were fuzzy, but it turns out that my mom had tried to kill herself. She didn't succeed and went back to the hospital. When I say "back" it's because she had been in the hospital recently. Jerald, her boyfriend, had her committed to the psych ward and my dad had gotten her out. Dad said, "Those doctors don't now shit." I bet he wished he had listened to the doctors when they said she was bipolar. Looking back I wished he would have listened and made her take her medicine. I'm not a psychiatrist, but alcohol and meth can't be good treatment plans for Bipolar Disorder.

I could go on and on with sad story after sad story, but I'm just trying to build a picture for you so that you can understand what makes me who I am today, and how some of who I am was shaped by what I saw and lived. Not for the, "oh my, what a sad childhood." I did have good times, too. My dad loved my sister and me, and we never, never questioned that. We also knew that we had two dads and we didn't claim the drunk, we claimed the Good Dad. The dad who tried to show my sister how to shape her eyebrows by using me as a mannequin and shaved off my entire left eyebrow in the process. The dad who would go to the store and buy pads for us, the dad who would tell us stories that made us laugh and laugh and laugh. We had a dad who didn't date women and refused to bring any women around us because he wanted us to feel secure that he was not going anywhere. The dad who had us convinced that if we ate too many potato chips it would lock our arms straight out for the rest of our lives, "potato chip lock" he would say. To this day, if I'm eating potato chips the thought enters my mind: "Jules, don't eat too many, you know what Dad says." Then I shake my head and laugh because I know it's not real. It's not real, right? The dad who was so sentimental that he cried at Hallmark commercials; seriously, have you ever seen an almost 300-pound man cry over a commercial? I have, many times! The dad and the ONLY person who held his arms out when I told him I was gay and said, "Little one, I know honey, I've always known and it means nothing to me. Gay or straight or whatever you are, you are my daughter and I love you." The dad who nursed me back from a nervous breakdown at 19 for over a year, picking me up out of bed and rubbing my head and listening to me cry and cry, screaming that I didn't want to be gay and didn't say a word other than, "shhh, it's okay Jules, Daddy's here." The dad who would have done anything for Jennifer and me. I just wish I knew before he died that he could not stop drinking and I wish I would have told him, "It's okay Pops, I've always known you couldn't stop drinking and I understand. Drinking or sober, you are my dad and I love you." When I get to heaven the first face I want to see is my dad so that I can tell him, "I love you Dad and its okay, your baby is here now."

Chapter 2
Genetics SUCK!

Over two years ago my partner and I were going through a rough spot in our relationship. After ten years together I cheated on her and it triggered memories that put me into a tailspin. I had suffered from depression and anxiety spouts most my life, and I knew that I just needed to see a psychiatrist and have them get me on some new medication. I had been on an antidepressant that helped for over seventeen years. It helped a little, I should say, but it never got rid of the anxiety or my mind racing. With the stress of my ten-year relationship on the brink I decided to go back in to my psychiatrist and try something different.

I was diagnosed with Bipolar II, with rapid cycling two years ago. When the psychiatrist told me I snickered. "I'm not bipolar. I'm successful, I don't drink, I don't do drugs, I've been in a relationship for over ten years; these are not signs of Bipolar." The psychiatrist just listened as I kept spouting my accomplishments: "I'm number one in the region for sales, I've never had anything but a leading evaluation at work, I support five people by myself, and my credit score is 815. I have the highest sales position you can acquire within an organization. You must have heard something I said wrong. My mother is bipolar, and I am nothing like my mother." He waited patiently for me to ask, "Are you sure?" He nodded. "Yes Jules, you have been suffering for a long time now, and it's time to let the right medication help you."

This was my worst nightmare: being diagnosed with Bipolar, regardless of the type. I grew up with crazy and I did everything I could to ensure that this did not rub off. "Dr. Rahman, why have I been as successful as I have been if I'm bipolar?" He replied, "Jules, Bipolar II is quite different from Bipolar I, the type everyone in the world is familiar with. The reason you have been so successful is because you have a high IQ and you have learned what is appropriate behavior and what is not. Plus, Bipolar II people have less severe mania symptoms than people with Bipolar I. Bipolar II does not produce psychosis or delusions. People who have Bipolar II usually retain somewhat sound judgment and usually do not engage in self-destructive behavior like Bipolar I people do. In fact, Bipolar II people usually have a sharpened intellect and have the ability to function with little sleep, and it contributes to Bipolar II individuals' success. With increased productivity and intellect non-bipolar II people can pale in comparison to Bipolar II peers. This is to say, Bipolar II can create a distinct advantage in the workplace, because it helps people to be maximally productive and get more things done than their peers. Bipolar II individuals are likely to be creative risk-takers, who can bring creative ideas to fruition. People have been diagnosed with depression or anxiety for years when they actually have Bipolar II. The medicines designed for depression and anxiety can make Bipolar II people worse, not better. Jules, you are a classic Bipolar II case, and I'm glad you came today because we are going to get you on the right medication to help slow the anxiety down. Aren't you getting tired?" Tired was not a word that described how drained and exhausted I was.

This was the curse, this was the family curse. The curse of Bipolar Disorder. I figured it out. But, with every bad is a good, just like with my dad. I want every person with Bipolar Disorder to understand that even though Bipolar sucks a lot of the time, we get to see life differently sometimes. For me it's like that one movie where the guy takes this pill and he is able to use 100% of his brain rather than 10%. So many opportunities open up that he never would have seen without the pill. You can feel on a deeper level than most, and that's both good and bad. For me my mind would run and run until it almost seemed like a light would come on in my brain and I had a moment of clarity of how to accomplish a task. I could see further down the road than most and with strategic sales, this is a godsend. I wrote these elaborate outlines that blacked out what I needed to do to accomplish a task and once the outline was complete, I was like a train that could not be stopped, even if it was a good idea to stop. I had a co-worker that would tell me, "Jules, slow down. You're selling too much and it's not going to end well." I knew she was right, but I couldn't control it.

Now, I'm not a psychiatrist and I know each case is different, but for me that is how it works. If you do research you will find that a lot of the best musicians, writers, salespeople, business people (my great-grandfather) were or are some type of bipolar or, as I like to call it, "some type of crazy." Do your own research, you will find the same thing. Here is a list of just a few you might recognize:

Famous People with some sort of Bipolar Disorder Actors & Actresses
Ned Beatty
Maurice Bernard, soap opera Jeremy Brett
Jim Carey
Lisa Nicole Carson
Rosemary Clooney, singer
Lindsay Crosby
Eric Douglas
Robert Downey Jr.
Patty Duke
Carrie Fisher
Connie Francis, singer and actress Shecky Greene, comedian

Linda Hamilton
Moss Hart, actor, director, playwright Mariette Hartley
Margot Kidder
Vivien Leigh
Kevin McDonald, comedian
Kristy McNichols
Burgess Meredith, actor, director Spike Milligan, actor, writer
Spike Mulligan, comic actor and writer Nicola Pagett
Ben Stiller, actor, director, writer David Strickland
Lili Taylor
Tracy Ullman
Jean-Claude Van Damme
Robin Williams
Jonathon Winters, comedian Catherine Zeta Jones

Artists
Alvin Alley, dancer, choreographer Ludwig Von Beethoven
Tim Burton, artist, director
Francis Ford Coppola, director
George Fredrick Handel, composer
Bill Lichtenstein, producer
Joshua Logan, broadway director, producer Vincent Van Gogh, painter
Gustav Mahier, composer
Francesco Scavullo, artist, photographer Robert Schumann, composer
Don Simpson, movie producer
Norman Wexler, screenwriter, playwright

Entrepreneurs
Robert Campeau
Pierre Peladeau
Heinz C. Prechter
Ted Turner, media giant

Financiers
John Mulheren
Murray Pezim

Miscellaneous
Buzz Aldrin, astronaut
Clifford Beers, humanitarian
Garnet Coleman, legislator (Texas)
Larry Flynt, publisher and activist
Kit Gingrich, Newt's mom
Phil Graham, owner of Washington Post

Peter Gregg, team owner and manager, race car driver Susan Panico (Susan Dime-Meenan), business executive Sol Wachtier, former New York State Chief Judge

Musicians
Ludwig van Beethoven, composer Alohe Jean Burke, musician, vocalist Rosemary Clooney, singer
DMX Earl Simmons, rapper and actor Ray Davies
Lenny Dee
Gaetano Donizetti, opera singer
Peter Gabriel
Jimi Hendrix
Kristen Hersh (Throwing Muses)
Phyllis Hyman
Jack Irons
Daniel Johnston
Otto Klemperer, musician, conductor Oscar Levant, pianist, composer, television Phil Ochs, musician, political activist, poet
John Ogden, composer, musician
Jaco Pastorius
Charley Pride
Mac Rebennack (Dr. John)
Jeannie C. Riley
Alys Robi, vocalist in Canada
Axl Rose
Nick Traina
Del Shannon
Phil Spector, musician and producer
Sting, Gordon Sumner, musician, composer Tom Waits, musician, composer
Brian Wilson, musician, composer, arranger Townes Van Zandt, musician, composer

Poets
John Berryman
C.E. Chaffin, writer, poet Hart Crane
Randall Jarrell
Jane Kenyon
Robert Lowell
Sylvia Plath
Robert Schumann Delmore Schwartz

Political
Theodore Roosevelt, President of the United States Abraham Lincoln, President of the United States

Robert Boorstin, special assistant to President Clinton
L. Brent Bozell, political scientist, attorney, writer
Bob Bullock, ex secretary of state, state comptroller and lieutenant
governer Winston Churchill
Kitty Dukasis, former First Lady of Massachusetts
Thomas Eagleton, lawyer, former U.S. Senator
Lynne Rivers, U.S. Congress

Scholars
John Strugnell, biblical scholar

Scientists
Karl Paul Link, chemist Dimitri Mihalas

Sports
Shelley Beattie, bodybuilding, sailing John Daly, golf
Muffin Spencer-Devlin, pro golf
Ilie Nastase, tennis
Jimmy Piersail, baseball player, Boston Red Sox, sports announcer
Barret Robbins, football
Wyatt Sexton, football
Alonzo Spellman, football
Darryl Strawberry, baseball
Dimitrius Underwood, football
Luther Wright, basketball
Bert Yancey, athlete

TV & Radio
Dick Cavett
Jay Marvin, radio, writer Jane Pauley

Writers
Louis Althusser, philosopher, writer Honors de Balzac
Art Buchwald, writer, humorist Neal Cassady
Patricia Cornwell
Margot Early
Kaye Gibbons
Johann Goethe
Graham Greene
Abbie Hoffman, writer, political activist Kay Redfield Jamison,
writer, psychologist Peter Nolan Lawrence
Frances Lear, writer, editor, women's rights activist Rika Lesser,
writer, translator
Kate Millet
Robert Munsch
Margo Orum

Edgar Allen Poe
Theodore Roethke
Lori Schiller, writer, educator Frances Sherwood
Scott Simmie, writer, journalist August Strindberg
Mark Twain
Joseph Vasquez, writer, movie director Mark Vonnegut, doctor, writer
Sol Wachtler, writer, judge
Mary Jane Ward
Virginia Woolf

On the other hand, bipolar of any kind has huge pitfalls, too. Each person with this disorder is different, but for me it turned into rage and anxiety. I couldn't control it. No matter how hard I tried, it was just a matter of time before I blew. Sometimes I felt in control and as I got older my control grew a bit, so I was left with the conclusion that in time I would be able to control the emotional roller coaster. Before I was diagnosed I was convinced that my rage, anxiety and totally uncontrolled emotions had to do with my childhood. It made sense, right? Anyone who was raised in such turmoil would have issues and my issues were products of that and not Bipolar Disorder.

As I look back on my life I saw a real pattern starting as a young adult. I would be fine for a bit and feel normal; I could go to the movies and enjoy the show. Then time would go and my mood would deepen, but it wasn't depression; it was tunneled thinking. When I was younger I would obsess about sexual conquests or about being tied down in a relationship and it haunted me and didn't allow me to find any true type of companionship. But as I got older I would switch this obsession to sales deals and I could go longer without blowing a lid. This was my idea of a safe obsession. These were the only two things that I would obsess about, so if nothing was going on at the time I went into tunnel vision and I would create some type of goal in my head that I had to achieve ASAP. I would try and control the obsession until I started to feel out of control. As soon as I felt really out of control I would explode, tell a woman I was dating that I didn't want to be with her, when in actuality wanted to but couldn't control the anxiety. This started the drama of crying, "Why don't you want to be with me?" and it would ease the pain, but it wouldn't be enough. I would then do something that would really mess things up in the relationship I was in, like having sex with one, two, three women in a weekend to erase the rage and the feeling of wanting to peel my skin off from my knuckles to my toes or pull out every eyelash I had. It was and is such a terrible feeling.

Once I sabotaged whatever it was that was going good in my life, depression and complete lack of self-worth was the finish line. At this point you could find me at a vitamin store searching for vitamin B12 or some sort of vitamin that would help eliminate the cloud. I refused, no matter how bad I felt, to give into drugs or alcohol. I had seen drugs and alcohol in action and I knew they didn't help anything. In some ways I'm glad that I had the childhood I did. If I had not seen what drugs and alcohol can do I might have turned to them for comfort.

When I entered my thirties, my obsession switched to sales and how to achieve a goal I set within my mind. This goal was something that would not let me rest until it was achieved, and then I would re-set it with another outrageous goal.

Throughout my life the situations would change, but it was a clear pattern. As I got older I could feel it coming on, and I tried to white-knuckle it and I grew better at it with each passing year. I learned to keep my life very calm, and I found a partner named Melissa, who was my calming blanket. I would feel it coming on and I would call her, and she had a way of easing the pain with a word or a hug and it helped.

But, even though I learned to blow up or obsess on safer situations and even though I tried to wrap my mouth with masking tape to ensure I didn't say something inappropriate or do something inappropriate, I still eventually did. I even turned to shopping, something I never was into before. My income started to grow over the six-figure mark and I found myself going on shopping sprees. It wasn't out of character to spend $10,000 in a day. Most people would go to the store when they saved up money for a couch, but oh no, not me. I went to the store for a couch, but would end up getting a couch, flat screen, bedroom set and a kitchen table, and in that same spree buy a brand new car. Going to the store to buy one item was not something I could do, and I still find it hard to this today.

Just try and imagine this cute little blonde woman (Melissa) trying to keep up with me, a woman that commanded force and instant action. I would say to the salesperson, "We'll take that and that, and do you have that? Okay, then we'll take three of those." It was like I was ordering donuts, not items over a thousand dollars apiece. Melissa would try and stop me, but after a while she would say, "Fuck it." She realized that I would eventually pay it off because I made such good money, so she started to get in the game with me. "Jules, let's get that over there, too." Being with me was such a drag most of the time that she eventually she knew the cycles and took advantage of them. Can you blame her? I sure can't.

So let's take a paragraph or two to examine the shifting behaviors of Melissa now, too, shall we? It'll be fun and uplifting. The shopping thing didn't take long for Melissa to change her tune. Oh, the first couple sprees she was, "No Jules, I don't need that really. That's nice, but too expensive." One or two shopping sprees and she knew the drill, and by the end of the third shopping spree she was ready. As soon as she could see I was starting to talk about buying something and I would get more and more agitated over the coming days she knew what was coming and she almost got giddy. Now my sprees have calmed down quite a bit and it has really, well, pissed her off. So recently we were going on a camping trip, the first in twelve years, and she kept telling me what we needed and we needed to discuss how much we wanted to spend on camping gear. She must have gotten really pissed with waiting for me, because one morning I checked the bank account. She had spent more than two thousand dollars on camping gear. Can you believe that? What can I say, she was a good student. I'm taking her in to see Dr. Rahman next week; we might have a mini Bipolar II on our hands.

It has taken about two years for me to really understand what hell I was living in, it really did. I became accustomed to it and as a human you have to adapt to survive. I was getting really good at white knuckling the situation, and as long as not too many things would change in my life I was okay. As okay as you can be, being bipolar II and not taking the right medicine.

I left Dr. Rahman's office that afternoon feeling like I could take a deep breath. "Okay, now you can figure this thing out and move the fuck on." Dr. Rahman gave me a script and I ran to the pharmacy to get it filled. I thought that this was the end of the line; I was cured. I got the script in my hand and I read the back. This medicine was for seizures – what the fuck? Man, was I wrong, this was just the beginning.

I felt worse in the next nine months that I had ever felt in my life. In the following nine months, Melissa would find me on the hallway floor sobbing; I lost my way above six-figure job because I couldn't think on this new medicine. The first time in my fucking life my sales dropped to average. Average! Are you kidding me? What I didn't realize was that I had pushed so many people around in my career. If you got in my way of a sale or an accomplishment or if I even thought you got in my way, I would destroy you. As it turns out, this turns people off and when you come down from crazy sales numbers to average you become, well, expendable. Average means you are a target, and my target was big because I had fucked so many people. When you start Bipolar II medications it takes a while to get used to them. This also means you don't think as fast or as clearly as you did before, so in the political arena at work I found myself in checkmate quite quickly and I was taken off the board.

Melissa was confused and even mad at times. "Jules, just get off this stuff and go back on the little antidepressant." I would reply, "No Melissa, he's right. I just need to figure this out; I need the right cocktail of medicine." I had begun reading about Bipolar II and realized quickly that Dr. Rahman was right. I started on two medicines, then he backed me off the antidepressant and I was only on one Bipolar or anti-seizure medicine. Then he added one more, and then another and it still was not right. I told him I couldn't work and I was crying all the time. I even cried while giving a presentation to one of my biggest potential clients. I could not control the tears. My numbers were down and when your numbers are down in sales and they pay you the kind of money they were paying me, companies feel like they are buying the rights to torment and ridicule you. I couldn't take it. It was like what my father had done to me as a child and I was in no place to handle it. My enormous wall was down and I was standing naked in the ring of fire.

Dr. Rahman asked me if I wanted him to write me a note for work to be off for a couple of weeks. Looking back I should have said yes; it might have saved my job. I began calling him every day. It reminded me of my nervous breakdown I had had when I was 19. "Oh no, not this again," I said to myself. Melissa had heard of my breakdown but used to shake her head. "Jules, it wasn't as bad as you thought. You are too strong to be as pitiful as you say you were." After nine months of torture she realized it might have been as bad as I said.

The night she found me on the floor crying and saying, "just take me to the hospital, I'm useless, I'm nothing, I'm a loser just like my dad said," I knew Dr. Rahman was wrong with the medication selection. A little wrong, but wrong is wrong. I pulled myself off the floor and told myself to knock this shit off, knock it off. I went in the next day and I looked terrible. I said, "Dr. Rahman, I need my antidepressant back." He responded, "Jules, antidepressants increase your cycles. This is not a good idea." I replied, "You might be right, but I want to try."

He wrote me a script that had helped me for the last twelve years. It was for a very small dose, but it did the trick. Even though my doctor was convinced I was wrong, he trusted me and together we came up with my cocktail. So a combination of the Bipolar medicine and one little antidepressant is my cocktail, and for the first time in my life I felt the clouds part and I could breathe. I was able to enjoy the weekends with my kids and Melissa. Before I would dread the weekends, because when my mind was not busy with work and sales strategies I couldn't relax. Weekends were horrible, tormenting and just downright terrible. I would do everything I could to not go into a rage and scare the shit out of my kids and Melissa.

I would see that my kids and Melissa were dealing with what I did as a child with my father. I hated it with every bone and fiber in my body, but I couldn't stop it. It was like a huge tsunami. These tsunamis were products of "relaxing" on the weekends. The weekdays I was following Melissa around obsessing about sales strategies and she would listen over and over and over again until I would say, "I got it," and run off. Melissa would turn around and I was gone. Then I would make a huge sale and start over again. But by the weekend I was screaming and throwing drawers or basically anything I could get my hands on. It was usually over a drop of chocolate on the counter or the living room not being picked up. You know, the things that were huge, horrible things that gave me the right to terrorize my family, right? Melissa was either dodging things being thrown at her or was being followed by me obsessing about some sales strategy I had. She did her best; she loved me and it was apparent. For the first time I began to understand my dad.

I lost my job and I was scared that this was going to send me over the edge. But every day that ended I was okay. Well, as okay as most people are when they lose a job that supported the entire family. I was worried, don't get me wrong, but I was an okay kind of worried. I decided to focus on working out; I had struggled with my weight my entire life and as I studied the new medicine I was on I read the words "weight gain" over and over again. Fuck that shit, I thought, no one is going to tell me that I'm going to gain weight. So I started to work out and really watch what I was eating. I refused to be fat, so I worked out.

I had tried to work out many times in my life, but if it wasn't on a team I could not get into a groove. My brain would start obsessing on something and my brain was too busy obsessing and I didn't have time to work out. Once the obsession would end I would lose my groove and I would start over again. After 10-15 times of this I gave up. But with the new medicines I found myself able to do it every day. Wow, I thought, this is cool.

My kids would ask me to play with them and I would say yes, as I had done in the past. But now I was really able to play. I used to say yes and play for three minutes and then run and find Melissa to obsess with her about some sales strategy. It wasn't real and I didn't enjoy playing; I did it because I thought I should. Now I do it and enjoy it as much as you can enjoy playing Barbie or sword fighter at the age of 37. It all became normal; I was becoming normal.

Normal had so many goods, but I worried about if I could sell any more when I got a new job. I worried about it, but not to the point of sweating and following Melissa around for hours on end.

I got a new job. It was several positions below where I had left, and that was okay with me. I didn't want the stress that I had just left. Funny that I felt it was stress when I started down the road of Bipolar II recovery. Before the diagnosis I would have said that work was what gave me life. Things were different now; I liked spending time with my family. I enjoyed things, really enjoyed things for the first time in my life. I could count on my emotions and I would not be constantly fighting them as I had before. Before I would reach a boiling point at work and I would throw a fit about something, and I would try and figure out how to get out of whatever situation my rage got me into. I was quite good at throwing people under the bus and demanding a raise when I was pushed up against the wall. Sales is one of the few professions where you are able to be a diva and get away with things. If you produced numbers you had a much wider leeway given. Sales, rock stars and movie stars allow divas, and I fit right in. One thing that always made me chuckle was watching my managers sit back and get all the accolades for the numbers that I was producing. They would try and brush it off and give credit to me, but you could see they also wanted to be rock stars. Who doesn't? But, at the end of the day they knew where the numbers where coming from, and so did I.

My new job was in small business sales, and it was a nice break. I sold to business owners that had very few employees and they were nice and fun to talk to. It was easy, really easy and I climbed my way up to the top of the leader board. I took a deep breath of relief – I could still sell. But, I was not able to reach the same level that I had once before. I would feel it coming on, the obsessive mind, racing thoughts that took to the top of the leader boarder and way beyond. And then it would settle down. It reminded me of having sex and being almost to climax and being so ready and excited and "beep". Not an earthquake of pleasure, just "beep". Good and bad, they come together, but this good outweighed the bad by far. I was still number one in the office, but only by a percent or two. I'd laugh when I saw the numbers and just shake my head and say, "the good outweighs the bad." Of course I would not let myself be anything but number one, but the margins were much, much, much, closer now.

I look at things differently now. When I see a successful person I wonder if it is mental illness or pure talent. Or is there a difference? Really, I ask: is there a difference? I'm really into Pink right now. I watch her tour videos as I work out and I can't help but wonder, is she bipolar II? Not meaning it to be bad, but good. Can people reach that amount of creativity and tunnel vision without mental illness? Imagine creating like she does without the help of seeing things differently. Does she see things differently, but has learned how to manage it? Or is she just talented and able to create and then walk away and go have dinner with her husband Carey without being totally obsessed? Or does she drive him crazy with, "Carey, listen to this, does that sound good, or wait, what about this." Is Carey her Melissa, and do we all need a Melissa, mentally ill or not? I don't know. Maybe you can be successful and not be obsessed, and I am just the unlucky one with the family curse. Can you be successful, really successful on the medicine? Bipolar is a scary word for most people, but for me it's been a blessing. I don't know the answers to my questions above and only time with tell. But my ultimate question is, why do we hide mental illness? Why do we hide ourselves? Why? Whether it's depression, anxiety, Bipolar Disorder, Tourette's or schizophrenia. Why can't we just be honest with ourselves and the people around us? "No, I can't go drinking with you guys because I take medicine for Bipolar II and I'm not supposed to drink on it. Sorry guys have fun and if you need a driver just give me a call." Maybe that day will come in our society when we are not trying to be perfect people without any problems.

Maybe, just maybe we are all a bit mentally ill and some are just more mentally ill than others? Maybe we would be shocked to know how many people are mentally ill, but wouldn't it allow us not to be so terrified if someone found out if we were mentally ill, too? But what if there were a reason people were such assholes to their spouses or a reason why people were addicted to drugs, alcohol or sex. Wouldn't it be better to de diagnosed with Bipolar II than just be an asshole? For me, I'll take the Bipolar flag and carry it willingly because it has come with some much needed relief in my life. So here it is: "I'm bipolar, regardless of the type. It's still bipolar and it's a scary word and it's a form of mental illness. It's okay if you are as well, welcome to the family."

Pink, if you are mentally ill, I welcome you to the family, too. Carey and Melissa would probably have a lot to talk about.

Chapter 3
The Early Years with Bipolar II

As I stated in my first chapter, I don't remember too much about my early childhood. I do remember some things, but to start from the beginning I have to rely on what my parents and my older sister had to say.

My mother has told me that I was a great baby. My older sister was a nightmare. She cried and fussed and was just a handful. This was the first and last time I was more charming than my sister, and I like to shove it in her face as often as I can. See, I'm charming still to this day. My mother was not on drugs yet and was in the same home as my father, so I bet things were nice when my parents weren't beating the shit out of each other. My mother used me like a doll and would dress me in all kinds of frilly dresses and laces and I would comply with her wishes. I do remember just being in love with her, my mother, that is. My mother was so beautiful, (the Glass curse) and I would stare at her for hours. My mother tells me that Jennifer was up and out of the house playing with other kids from dusk until dawn, but most days I was always by her leg looking up.

I guess our tradition was to cook dinner together, and I would sit on the counter and just ask all kinds of questions. "Mom, what's that and what do you do with that, and how is that grown?" Apparently I had an extensive vocabulary at a very early age, and my parents were quite proud of that. I wanted to learn, I wanted to learn with everything that I had. I had no desire to play with other children. I gained much pleasure being around the adults. Adults knew much more than children did. Children were childish and boring and I would rely on adults as my playmates.

One of the stories that you can hear my mom tell a lot is the first day of kindergarten. Dorothy Hamel was popular at the time and I wanted my hair like hers. I begged and begged my mother, but she would not have it. I had thick, long, beautiful straight blonde hair and it was like a prize that my mother liked showing off. I would ask every day, "Mom, can I get my hair cut like Dorothy Hamel?" "No Jules, your hair is too beautiful." So you can imagine the surprise when I came in from the back door with a huge blonde ponytail in one hand and scissors in the other. She still gets pissed talking about it now; I truly do not believe she has forgiven me for that. But, when the first day of kindergarten arrived I had my Dorothy Hamel hair and I thought I looked good.

I finished off the hairstyle with a silk blouse that buttoned down the front and at the wrists. The shirt was blue and I was convinced it was a business shirt. I wanted to be a businesswoman, so I should wear a business shirt. All the other kids came prancing in with backpacks and I came in cautiously looking over my competition with my back briefcase. No backpack for me: too childish. I had to have a briefcase. Even as a child I danced to a different beat and I didn't give a shit when I was that age. It took time to become ashamed of my differences.

All the kids were conversing with each other as the teacher rang a bell and asked the children to sit in a circle and introduce themselves. Blah, blah, I thought, let's get to this. Finally she said she was going to read a book in circle time. I looked at my mom; I was so excited. I could read. I was only four and the youngest kid in the class, but I could read with the best of them. Driving my mother nuts about going to school had nudged her to request that I start kindergarten a year early.

So it began, the story, that is: "Once upon a time," she started and then I raised my hand. "Yes, Jules," replied Mrs. Short. "Yes Mrs. Short, the inflection on once upon a time is off, I would like to read the book." With that I stood up and grabbed the book from my teacher's hand and began reading the book to the children. My teacher was appalled!

My interruption in the class earned my mother a seat in the principal's office and earned me an evaluation. My mother has never told me what they found, only that they wanted me to skip another grade. My mother thought that one year ahead was enough, so I stayed in kindergarten at four and continued to drive Mrs. Short nuts for the remainder of the year. Mrs. Short was probably thrilled, don't you think? God, what a pain in the ass I was. Now I'm a complete delight, though.

I wish I were able to remember more about my mother before she started doing drugs. My mother to me was so out of control and unable to squeeze any happiness out of the simplest things in life. It took partying all night or painting the kitchen at three in the morning to get a smile out of her. On the other side of her emotion was raw and yucky. Yucky isn't a word that a 37- year old says but that's what I used to think as a child and it just came back. Yucky. When you love someone, really love someone and you see that person in so much pain... not the emotional pain of losing a job or a pet dying, but the kind of pain losing a child would produce or walking in on a partner that you are deeply in love with having sex with your best friend. This is that kind of pain I would see my mom in. If I asked you to take that kind of pain and put it into your mom's heart and then blink back to when you were ten, I believe you would think it was yucky too. Maybe yucky is an okay word, even at 37?

I started my academic life with such passion and enthusiasm, but that started to wean quickly. I can't remember exactly when it happened, but eventually I started to hate school. "Hate" is a word I take very seriously. My sister says, and I agree with her, that every time you say the word "hate" it makes the devil smile. That has always been so profound and true for me; the word "hate" is an ugly word. But I did. I hated school. So I started to dream in school to get through the day, I mean really dream. I would create these families in my mind and all these wonderful things that would happen to us. My disassociation from my family and my life was so real to me that I began to live in this fantasy world. I had a lover when I was in my twenties who was a psychologist, and she never believed in multiple personalities. I always told her I could see someone disassociating to that level for survival. Now don't flip out, I don't have multiple personalities. But I could see how it could happen. I never left reality, but if I zoned out, I would experience pleasure and comfort in my fantasy family and it was enough for me.

If I have to say why I zoned out so much, it was because when I was younger I was so eager to learn. I was always ahead of the class and they were never teaching something that I didn't already know. So my mind would wander and by the time they were surpassing my knowledge I was too busy creating this perfect family life in my head. Makes sense that after a while I was behind, and when I'm not good at something I don't focus on it, so I didn't focus on school and my grades were about average.

Good or bad with my pretend family, it gave me comfort. But I didn't learn much in school. To this day, if you start talking about fiction, non-fiction, verbs, nouns or history I clam up because I will be lost. Knowledge does not constitute intelligence; it just means that you know a lot by listening to others or reading words by others. The core factor for intelligence is seeing a problem and the ability to fix the problem. That cannot be taught, and it is what it is. Sales is problem solving. If you can find the problem and you have a product that will fix the problem, you have a sale. It's that simple. You can take all the courses and self-help seminars you want, but that's the key. Send the publisher $250, they will take their cut and send me the rest. I just gave you the golden apple. No need to go to those seminars that spout that they have the key to being a great salesperson. What they do have is the ability to take your money and teach the same thing differently.

I spent my days in school dreaming about my family in my head and waiting for the bell. After school was sports and that was worth the wait. I always showed up wide-eyed and bushy- tailed. My wonderful disposition didn't leave me many fans my age or older, but coaches would be nice to me so I would stay on their teams. At an early age I felt that the only way to get people to like me was to do something for them, and as a young child it was doing well in sports.

"Come on girls," my father said abruptly, "let's go visit your mother". My mom had been in the hospital again for a couple of days after her suicide attempt and we had asked our dad if we could see her. At the hospital, my father walked up to the counter. "I'm here to see Jean Alexander, my wife." His wife, I thought, I thought they were divorced. In fact they were, but my father still felt like she was his. It always felt like my father was heartbroken with the breakup, but I didn't really know until that moment. I grabbed his hand and looked up at him and smiled. I knew he could fix it, I knew he could get Mom home.

I missed my mom, but I was glad I didn't have to worry when the sun would go down. That was when men would show up at our house and they would try and be nice to me, but I wasn't stupid. I knew they were there to fuck my mother. I would try desperately not to go to bed. I would pray, "Please God, don't let me get tired." But eventually I did, and that meant the adults would do what adults did. Well, at least what they did at my house: fuck, and very loudly at that. It was so disturbing to me, it haunted me, the sounds. I can't find the right words to tell you how I felt. It was as if a funnel was being turned on inside my chest and my childhood was being siphoned out of me an ounce at a time. Those nights I would not sleep I would just sit up in my bed with my knees to my chest and sob. Every night was the same. I would fall off to sleep with these words: "Where are you, God? I need you."

"Jean. Jean! Jean, come on your girls are here," my father said. My mom's eyes barely opened. She looked like a zombie. She had this gown on, with blue slippers and a white robe. It took several seconds for her to respond and when she all she could get out was, "Hi." My dad's face was changing and I could see he was getting angry. I looked at Jennifer and Jennifer looked at me. Jennifer was tearing up, which was not a daily occurrence as it was with me, and my dad noticed. "Fuck this," he said. Come on girls. We followed behind and I wondered what he was going to do, but I knew he would fix it. And he did, or so I thought.

"What do you have her on?" my father asked. These were always comical situations to watch with my dad confronting men, because it was almost like they looked like his bitches standing next to him. He was so big and powerful and I never ever saw a man my dad did not intimidate. It was fun, in sick way, to see others be a bit frightened of him. "Mr. Alexander, we have her sedated." "Sedated? She's a zombie, asshole." The doctor looked down to gain composure and tried to explain that my mother had been hysterical and that she needed to be sedated. He believed she needed to remain in the hospital so that she could be stabilized on the right Bipolar medicine.

You could have heard a pin drop. I knew what he was thinking and

I started to smile. Looking back of course it was the worst thing that you could do for my mother, but it felt like we were a family again. My dad stormed out of the doctor's office. "Come on girls." He headed for my mother's room. When we got to the door he picked her up in his arms and said, "Come on Jean, I'm taking you home." My dad took all of us to his apartment and nursed my mom back from her depression. He was so thoughtful and so caring and so loving toward her. My father was able to keep his anger in check when a crisis was happening, something I would understand later in life. But, all I knew then was that for three weeks I would go to school, come home and nobody was drunk, yelling or fighting and I didn't have to worry about the sun going down.

Summer was starting and my father managed to become his old self and started to terrorize my mother. He belittled her and took any self-respect that she had and shoved it right back up her ass. So she left, and I don't blame her. Being okay and being loved by my father at that age was impossible. My father was the worst thing that could have ever happened to my mother. She needed the opposite of my dad. They loved each other, but their demons did not mix well together.

After those three weeks of glorious life (aww childhood memories) all three weeks of them. I will cherish them always. We went to Mexico for the summer. My mother had recently broken up with her rich attorney boyfriend, and apparently he felt bad or wanted my mom out of his hair. I have a feeling it was out of his hair; he wasn't someone who would take any glorious light from Jesus. Jesus is safe from that fucker stealing any of his kindness away.

Jerald was a jerk in the highest form, but when my mom is in a relationship and somewhat content it's kind of, well, normal. I do remember waking up on Saturdays at Jerald's house with my mom making pancakes in the shape of an "A." That was cool. Jerald had a daughter. I forget her name, but I liked her. She was kind of strange, like me, so we got along. Jennifer on the other hand thought we were both crazy bitches and tried to avoid us at all costs. Jennifer was too popular and cool to be seen with us dorks.

When no one was looking she'd wrap her arms around me and tell me she loved me. I always liked that. She still does it to this day and I still like it. Jennifer is the complete polar opposite from me in almost every way. The only thing we have in common is our parents and the fact that we love each other and would move mountains to make sure either one of us didn't get hurt. So, in the sister realm I lucked out, thanks God!

I don't know what happened, but one day, while we were living with Jerald, my mom started drinking. Really drinking. Not the, "oh what a nice moon tonight Jerald, let's have a glass of wine and talk on the patio" kind. It was the "let me see how much I can drink and still wake up in the morning" kind of drinking. I actually have the exact amount a woman at 5'7 and 120 pounds can drink without dying. Let me run and get the numbers, I'll be right back. Okay, I'm back. The correct amount is: a fucking ton! She was an athlete of alcohol and she was at the tiptop of her game at this time in her life.

When I changed schools to Jerald's county I was upgraded. These kids had parents with Mercedes and BMWs and all the other fancy cars rich people drive. Even though my father's family had a lot of money we did not live in that manner. When you live off your family for years the money gets smaller and the urgency to work gets bigger, and this multiplies rapidly if no intervention performed. An intervention was not performed, in case you were wondering. But, at Jerald's house I felt like I fit in. I liked living in a huge luxurious house on the beach in Miami, I felt like somebody going to that new school. In my closet I had a row of alligator shirts in every color with khaki pants and K-Swiss shoes. I wore the same thing every day, but in different colors. I picked out a cool outfit, and to make it easier I wore it every day, just in different colors. I do that today, too. When I like something, I like something, no reason wasting my time finding another outfit I like. What's the use when there are so many colors for that one outfit, right? Plus, the added benefit is that it makes getting ready in the morning easier. You might not have a lot of friends, but who cares if you save seven minutes of contemplation every morning? Who needs friends when you have an extra seven minutes every day? I need to write self-help books, I believe I have a gift.

Jerald was intelligent and I enjoyed talking with him. He made me think and contemplate decisions and consequences. "Jules, I got you something." "What is it?" "I bought these authentic Chinese clothes that kids in China wear to school on my trip for you." "Cool, they really wear these to school?" Jerald went into this dissertation of the Chinese culture and how we could learn a great deal from them, and how the intellect level in China was far greater than here in States. He then told me that here in this country these types of clothes were worn as pajamas. I peeled my clothes off and put these silky green Chinese clothes on and took my butt to bed. When I woke up in the morning I had decided that it would be a good decision to wear them to school as well. Jennifer about fell off her chair when I announced what I was going to be wearing to school that day. I didn't care; I was wearing them. My mom said it was okay and I was off to school.

Pause, pause on my computer as I try to find the words: DON'T YOU EVER LET YOUR CHILDREN DO THIS. If you do, it will be the worst day at school in their entire academic career, trust me. "Embarrassment" is not the correct word for this. In fact, the word does not exist. JUST DON'T DO IT. "Can I wear traditional Chinese clothes to school, Mom/Dad?" Run and get this book and re-read this paragraph, enough said!

"Jules! Jennifer! Get out of bed; it's time to go to school! Get up girls," my mother slurred. It was half past eleven at night and we just went to bed three hours earlier. Jennifer and I both stumbled into the hall at the same time. We looked at each other, seriously confused.

Have you ever smelled an alcoholic? The smell is very distinct; it's a mix of body odor and alcohol along with a toxin that emanates off the alcoholic's skin. To this day I can tell if someone is high and what drug they are on and if they are an alcoholic, regardless of whether they have had anything to drink that day. My mother that night was roasting with the alcoholic smell. She was drinking when we went to bed, but she must have put it into high gear because she was convinced it was time for us to get ready to go to school. At first we tried to play it off as a joke. Once again Jennifer and I tried not to make our mom feel bad. "Mom, that's funny! You had us going. Okay, were going back to bed." My mom tried to stand still, but her body kept rotating in a slight circle. She looked up and then down and then at each of us. "Don't tell me it's not time to go to school, you girls know it's time and you're fucking with me," she said. Jennifer was concerned. Most of the time she had such a "whatever" personality that it scared me, and I started to cry. Jennifer was my rock; if she was worried, that made me worried.

My mom turned to go downstairs and fell on the floor and started to growl, cry, sob, I don't know. It sounded like an animal and she looked like a crazy woman. Jennifer and I ran to each other and held each other. Jennifer's hand covered her mouth like she was trying not to let any crazy get into her mouth. My mom worked her way up and down the stairs to our rooms and started throwing drawers and hangers of clothes on the floor saying, "GET READY FOR SCHOOL," in what sounded like a satanic voice that you would hear on a movie. Jennifer and I each grabbed an outfit and put it on as fast as we could. Then we grabbed our backpacks and we ran out the door with our mom still yelling at us.

It was pitch black when the door closed behind us. We didn't know what to do. We lived on a steep hill and if we weren't careful, a car could come up the hill and hit us. Jennifer grabbed my hand and said, "Let's go sit by the garden until she passes out." I remember crying as hard as my little body would allow me to cry. Jennifer on the other hand did not; she just held me. We said nothing. Morning came and my mother was passed out on the living room floor. We showered and got our clothes on and went to school. At school, after a night like that – and I've had quite a few – was weird. My senses were always heightened and I felt like everything was really loud and that everybody knew. Everybody knew that I was such a loser that I could not fix my family, and my chin would always find my chest on days like these, as if I had something to be sorry for. The only thing I was looking forward to was seeing my sister, and that didn't come until after school, so I'd just have to wait.

I don't know how long or what took place, but my mother ended up in something that was either a hospital or rehab; it looked like a hospital to me. My grandmother and aunt flew in from Tacoma, Washington. My aunt recently had gotten off of heroin and was living with my grandparents until she got back on her feet. I was relieved. My grandmother was just as beautiful as her 20-something-year old daughters, and she was a bitch. Let's just be frank, shall we? I feel like I know you now, since you know my whole life. She wasn't a very nice lady; she always had something mean to say to make sure you knew she was smarter than you.

My grandmother stayed a week. A week! Are you kidding me? Your daughter is having a nervous breakdown and you can't seem to find the time in your schedule to stay more than a week? Now, let me tell you, I'm not a superb mother. Melissa has Mother of the Year taken and I'm way far down the line, but I am a good mom. There is no way in HELL I would leave my child in the condition my mother was in. I don't care what I would have to do; I would not leave my child. There would be no excuse that would be acceptable to leave my child in the state my mother was in.

Somehow it was decided that my aunt Sara would stay at the house with us and take care of us. My aunt was fun and full of life. She looked like my mother, so I instantly felt close to her. She didn't drink and was, well, refreshing. Even though I missed my mom and I worried about her I was doing okay.

My sister and aunt Sara really hit it off; they always have. I, on the other hand, was harder to take. I didn't know how to be close to someone. I have never known how to be close to people, related or not. At that time I only knew how to be close with my sister, and my sister liked her, so I guess I thought it was okay if I liked her, too. A couple of days later we visited my mom and she looked better. We went to a circle and talked, and I called it "circle talk". Everyone thought that was funny. It felt good to make everyone laugh. Jerald came and he smiled and held my mother, and it looked like it was going to be okay. After the visit we piled in his brand new 7-series BMW and stopped off at this cool restaurant. Jerald always knew the really interesting places to go in Miami.

The day passed and another came, and I was coming home from school, skipping and thinking that everything was going to be okay.

I went into the kitchen and opened up the pantry to get a snack when I heard something. It was a familiar noise, and I immediately walked into the pantry and shut the door. The pantry was bigger than most people's walk-in closet. I stood there, trying to figure out what I was hearing. My blood raced and I was scared, really scared. My mom is going to kill herself if she finds out, I thought, but I have to tell her. Maybe it was nothing. I opened the door and looked through the crack. I'm an adult now, I can be frank: yes, my aunt and Jerald were having sex. Wow, what a winner sister there, huh?

I tried to get back into the pantry without them seeing. I didn't know what to do; I was nine, for fuck's sake, come on! How much can one child take, people? I slipped as I was backing up and I jumped up and ran to the back of the pantry and hid as small as I could in the corner. The funny noises they were making stopped and it went silent. I could hear them walking toward me.

I will never forget her face at that moment as long as I live; I have never ever seen such a mean evil woman in my life. The door opened and Sara appeared. "Jules! You didn't see anything. No one would believe you anyway. You wouldn't want to hurt your mother more, would you?" I looked at the potato chips I had knocked down as I fell to the ground and replied, "No."

I sat with those words my aunt said to me for what seemed like a lifetime. Jennifer was really having fun with Sara and I didn't want to ruin her fun and safety; we didn't get too much of that at that time. One night Jerald, Sara and Jennifer went to a concert and crashed his precious BMW. They never explained to me what happened, but it scared Jennifer and I was pissed. Jennifer was my everything, and Jerald and Sara had put her in harm's way. I was livid. In the next day or two we went to visit my mother. Sara kept giving me the eye, and I was confused. I didn't know what to do. I told my mother what I saw that day the best way I could at nine. She was upset, but actually comforted me. Did I do the right thing? My next memory of my mother was her naked on the couch after she had tried to commit suicide; she had gotten out of the hospital and Jerald broke up with her. Sara was right? I did hurt her more?

Jules Alexander

Chapter 4
Mexico/Dad's House

As a parting gift and two hospital visits later, we were off to Mexico for the summer on Jerald's dime. No dad, no Jerald, so no drama; just girl time to relax and recuperate. We went to Puerto Vallarta and other little cities up and down the coast of Mexico. It could have been a blast if my mom hadn't been drunk the WHOLE time.

Jennifer and I were so excited – what kid wouldn't be? I was especially excited because I had my two most favorite people with me: my mom and Jennifer. Jennifer always had friends around, so having her to myself was a big treat to me. I think my mom was sober on the way to the hotel, but that was the last we saw of sober Mom. I truly don't believe my mom even remembers most of the trip. She never talks about this time, and it makes me feel like I'm crazy. Jennifer doesn't either, and I wonder sometimes if that is not the best way to handle it.
We were in Mexico for quite a while, long enough that I started to pick up the language. Jennifer thought it was neat that I could speak with the locals. I don't know how I did it. I was young and probably able to adapt easier. Jennifer and I would wander the streets and see what was out beyond the tourist areas. "Jennifer, I want to parasail." We went back to the hotel to get into Mom's purse and make sure she had a pulse. All was good, so off to the beach we went.
The Mexican men would check Jennifer out in a weird way; Jennifer was twelve and looked like she was seventeen. She still had a young aura, but her body didn't match. The guys hooked me up to the parasail and I was off. They probably went in the normal route, but when it came to getting me down they couldn't. I wasn't heavy enough, but the guys wanted the money and let me do it anyways.
It took a couple of hours, but they got me down and all I could think about was that I was not down there to protect Jennifer if those men wanted to hurt her. I felt selfish for choosing to be up here and not down there. When I got down, all Jennifer could do was laugh; she thought it was hilarious that I was so scared. We laughed and went to the pool and ordered soda until we were in a diabetic coma.
We did so much fun stuff: we water-skied in the ocean with the sharks. What dumb asses we were. We hired a couple of local men to take us horseback riding one day. When they appeared with the horses we noticed they had blood on their lower extremities, and they were just worn out and sweating. These horses were not in good shape. We asked for our money back, but they refused. One

of the men had money in his hands and I grabbed it and said, "Come on, Jennifer." We ran as fast as we could and when we looked back they were gone. Stupid, stupid – what was I thinking?

My spontaneous bipolar actions were starting to rear their heads. I can't say why they didn't chase us; maybe because we were so close to a resort they would have gotten in trouble for it. I don't know, but I'm thankful.

When I came to the hotel one afternoon a guy was casing our room and looking at my mother through the window. Even at the age of nine I knew he was thinking about raping her. I told Jennifer that I wanted to leave the hotel, and in a drunken stupor we got Mom into a taxi and asked the driver to take us to another hotel. I noticed that the taxi driver was now looking at my mom with the same eyes. Two in one day. Beauty had so many wonderful benefits and I thought, I sure hope I'm ugly when I grow up. I was starting to be able to read people, and I didn't like what I was reading. Jennifer was usually caught in her own world, and that was probably good for her. I nudged Jennifer and said, look. The guy was a total pervert and I knew a nine-year old, twelve-year old and a drunken woman were no match for him. The wheels were turning in his head and I could feel that he was thinking about raping my mother and maybe all of us. He asked questions like, "Where is your father?" I can't remember exactly, but they were self-serving questions. It was at this moment that I switched from a child to my mother to a mother to my mother. I found my voice and presence, the voice and presence that would save me in the years to come.

The taxi slowed down and stopped at a busy intersection I told my sister to get Mom. I grabbed the bags. We jumped out of the car. The childhood ounces that were being siphoned from my chest had now turned into gallons. It was at that moment I knew if someone was going to take care of everybody, it was going to have to be me.

My mother had a younger sister named Ginger. From what I was told they had been tied at the hip when they were growing up. I remember my mother telling me about a time during her teenage years: She and her friends were going to Tijuana to party. Ginger wanted to go, but my mother told her she was too young. As their car pulled up to the border they heard a thumping in the trunk. It was loud enough that the border patrol heard it and made them pull over. Yep, you guessed it. Ginger had hid in the trunk to go partying with her older sister. Of course the border patrol made them call their parents, and my granddad went to get the girls. Ginger was so pissed because she thought it was going to be her big party night. But she had such a way to her that she convinced my granddad to take them anyway. He did and they had clean fun; not what a teenage were looking for, but fun nevertheless. I remember meeting Ginger two times in my life. They were both a blast. The first time was when my mother cooked all day for Thanksgiving, and Ginger and my uncle Kenny came over. They didn't show up until late and they didn't bring anything with them. My mother said something funny about this, and they laughed and laughed. I can't remember what was said, but it was very apparent that they loved each other. Once the meal began the laughter really started. My mother burned, over-salted and either overdid or underdid just about everything. Ginger made sure she took every stab that she could. She obviously thought that she was one clever woman with all the remarks. Uncle Kenny and my Dad kind of laid back; they knew this was going to get ugly real fast.

Finally the dinner was done, and from what I remember it was about as terrible as it could be. I felt bad for my mom because I think she really tried. "Would anybody like some pie?" my mother said in an almost a June Cleaver voice. My aunt then said, "Did you bake any of them?" to which my mother said no. Ginger said, "Then of course I will like a piece." Mom asked whether she wanted it with whipped cream or without. My aunt said, "With, please." Next thing I knew Mom slammed my aunt right in the face with a cherry pie. I was shocked and just froze. My mother and aunt laughed their asses off, and then the pie fight was on. Everyone got into the game and I got my uncle Kenny really good and then hid in the closet to avoid being retaliated upon. Uncle Kenny was my favorite. He was the one that found the mini business brief case I had in kindergarten. He was a businessman and I loved him.

The other time was when my auntie Ginger got us roller-skates. Most adults would have only bought skates for the kids, but she bought a pair for herself as well and we skated our asses off. She was so beautiful in more ways than just outer beauty. She was very special and she and my mother evened each other out. My auntie Ginger was my mother's soothing blanket, like Melissa is to me now, and I think it worked the other way around as well.

I remember hearing the ring. It was about 10pm. My father answered. He hung up and told my mother that her sister had just died at Seattle Hospital. My mom's scream curdled; it was raw and primitive and it knocked all muscle control from my mother's body, and her carcass slapped the floor. My mother was never the same after that day.

In my opinion my auntie Ginger was murdered by a cult. This cult took my aunt and took my mother. That is how I feel. My mom died too that day. It completely changed the direction of her life, and the new path was a clear-cut self-destructive one.

When we returned from Mexico my mom, Jennifer and I moved

back into the house on Pebble Place. The Jerald aura was gone and I was happy to be back home. My sister was around thirteen now, and she was starting to fill out even more. Jennifer had a shape like my grandma Jean. My father would say that she was a big girl. Not fat by any means, just big-boned. My mother was 5'7, but a small 5'7, little bones.

"Jennifer, get out here and vacuum this living room." My mother was in one of the cleaning sprees she would get in, and it was tiring to watch. Jennifer appeared, but she did not appreciate being summoned. "Do it yourself, Mother!" My mother reached back to slap my sister and the moment her hand landed my sister struck back with a slap that juggled some of my mother's brains. My mom was shocked, and for the first time I believe she was scared of my sister. Jennifer went back to her room. She was tired of my mother and she didn't want to deal with her. She had been hurt by her too many times. Jennifer was done. She called my dad and he came and got her. I was now left with my mother.

Begging the sun not to go down became a ritual with me. I loved my mom with all of me; I was a mommy's girl. She didn't take my sister leaving well and went back to drinking, and I think it was at this time that meth knocked and entered into my mom's life. I didn't want to leave my mother, and I was scared of my dad. But it wasn't long until I couldn't take it anymore; I missed my sister too much. My dad came and got me too.

I believe that every person has an emotional tank. Good events, like falling in love or getting a good job fill up the tank. Bad events like falling out of love and losing a job deplete the tank. Each person is also given the ability to handle situations bad and good, and different events have different amounts of positive and negative that affects the tank. Too many tragedies at one time cause the tank to go empty, and when it does you will lose your mind. What I think is intriguing is that so many people don't realize how easy it is for a tank to get to empty. If your tank gets too low, you don't have much you can take before you are back on empty again.

I started this book with the idea of explaining Bipolar II and I've ended up re-living my childhood in the process. I've spent many hours with old tapes that I've placed in storage long ago. I haven't been sleeping well. I can't concentrate at work and I have had several cry- hangovers in the process. When I was diagnosed with Bipolar II, Dr. Rahman said something to me that has stuck with me: "Jules, you could talk for hours and it would not help you. You have a chemical imbalance that cannot be helped with psychotherapy." (love that word ,don't you, "psychotherapy") "Once you are balanced, then it would be a good idea to do so." I've been to dozens of therapists, and they don't seem to help a fucking thing.

I end up feeling worse than when I started. I had one therapist tell me, "It's amazing that you or your sister didn't end up living under a bridge and drinking yourself to death." I thought that was kind of harsh, because even though our parents were fucked up they loved us, and I'm so thankful for this. I've realized one thing: that I didn't really know when I started. I always knew my father loved me, but I questioned my mother's love. As I stated in the beginning, I don't remember much of my early childhood. But making myself look back has helped me understand my mother did love me and does love me. That alone has been worth all the cry-hangovers.

I remembered my cat named "Bigfoot" that had six toes, and became pregnant, that slut. She gave birth to three kittens. My mother came and got me out of bed when she was about to deliver, and she explained everything to Jennifer and me about what was happening. I was amazed, and I realized my mother had gone through all of that to have me. I remembered her decorating my room with green and pink, and how careful my mother was with making sure I was involved in the process. If you were able to see my daughter's room today you would find the same green and pinks in her room. Weird. I remembered her painting a whole wall in the spare room with all the letters in the alphabet, and she would sit for hours as I asked questions about letters and words and what they meant. I remembered a stuffed animal named "Pinky Tusk A Dero" and how careful my mom was to make sure to ask if "Pinky" wanted to come with us when we were leaving the house. I remembered going to the desert for a camping trip and looking up at my mother with her beautiful hazel eyes, and she picked me up and placed me on her hip and said, "Do you know I love you, Jules?" I say that to my kids today and I thought I came up with it. It was my mom who started that, and I remembered that. Every night before I go to bed I ask each of my children the same question and it brings a smile each time I say it. I say it so much now that even before I get it out my oldest will say, "Yes Mom, I know you love me, now can I go play a video game?"

My mother's tank went to empty in her twenties, and she was unable to fill it back up. My father's rage and constant belittling mixed in with a loveless mother, Bipolar I, and topping it off with her sister and best friend and comforting blanket dying did her in. The sad thing is that her tank is still so low. I still wish I could fill her tank, as I had wished I could have as a child.

My mother's last heartbreak before her tank went empty was the heartbreak that Jerald caused. This man broke her heart along with other things. He was an awful man and I didn't go into detail because I just didn't have the strength at the time I was writing about him. But, let your mind wander into the black abyss and you will find Jerald's actions. Through all of this you could always find my mother saying, "What comes around goes around, and it does no good to allow hate into your heart." What a weak bitch, I would think, and it gave me comfort when my father told me a story about Jerald.

My dad's temper came to good use one night as he waited for Jerald in the dark of Jerald's office parking lot. From what my dad told me, Jerald didn't feel real good physically after he came into the parking lot to get into his 7-series BMW. Aw right dad, I thought when he told me that story, but nothing compared to the day I walked into a pharmacy in Miami.

It was in the afternoon and just another gorgeous day in beautiful Miami. I headed to the pharmacy to get my prescription filled and I heard a voice that stopped me in my tracks. I couldn't place it, but I knew it was familiar. When I walked up to the counter I saw a homeless person smelling of BO begging for drugs. What a strange sight, I thought; like the pharmacist is going to say, "Sure asshole, here is some oxies, have a nice day." I giggled a little when I thought about this. I proceeded to the other side of the counter to go to the un-crazy side when I saw an old briefcase with the initials GWR. I looked up at this stinky homeless drug addict and saw Jerald W. Reese. I was so shocked that I had to catch myself from my knees giving in. "Gerald?" I said. Why I acknowledged him I don't know, but the man looked up and it was Jerald. He had lost his practice and everything he owned, and now was a street drug addict. "It's Jules, Jerald." He looked up and wanted a hug, and I put both my hands up to tell him to back off. I walked away but before I left and I went to the soda isle and purchased a Squirt soda. I walked back to the homeless man and said, "Here. I know you like these, Jerald." With that I walked out and thought about my mom's statement, and it became much more profound. I know this is not Christian, but I smiled as I entered my car and thought to myself, "You deserve it, asshole. Enjoy your Squirt."

Chapter 5
The Beginning of the Sadness

My dad moved out of the apartment to a three-bedroom condo closer to where our schools were. He could tell that I missed my mom and that I was heartbroken. He tried to comfort me the best he could. I think he kept his anger in check because he knew I just couldn't take it. One day turned into two, and it was becoming normal. I thought as a child would think: maybe Dad's not going to blow up anymore. I started to feel more comfortable; Jennifer was with me and there was no sign of Bad Dad. My dad tried to decorate the house to make us feel more at home and to be honest, he needed some help. The walls were all white and no paintings, just the essentials, but it was my new home.

Almost every night we had boiled chicken in water and teriyaki sauce. It was good, don't get me wrong, but: every night! The cupboards were always bare and if you wanted anything to eat you had to get on your bicycle and ride to the 7'11. My dad brought the chicken home every night and made it. We never had groceries because my dad "sleep ate". Have you heard of it? It's hilarious. He would be totally asleep, and if there was any food in the house he would find it and eat it all. From time to time I would ask him for $100.00 to go grocery shopping, and I would ride my bike to the Safeway and spend $99.99 on groceries and take several trips to get it all home on the bike. I would put it away and look at the cupboards. It made me feel like it was more of a home. Then I would wake up to find that every piece of food was gone in the house and my dad would not remember it. "Dad, you ate all the food again!" My dad would look at me surprised: "I did? Oh." I would get so disappointed because of how hard it had been to get this all accomplished on a Saturday.

I was so pissed one day that I went to Jennifer's room to vent. She said, "Jules, next time you go grocery shopping we will chain the refrigerator and cupboards shut so he can't get to the food." Brilliant, I thought. The following Saturday I jumped my happy ass on my bike and went shopping with the $100.00 I got from my dad. Night came and Jennifer and I locked everything up with a couple of bicycle chains. We waited. We sat giggling up in Jennifer's room as we heard my father get up. My father was very ritualistic with his times. He started to drink at 3pm and finished his vodka bottles, three joints and his boiled chicken; then off to bed. He would be up two or three hours after he went to bed to finish off any of the chicken that remained, and off to bed again. This night though, the house was full of groceries with chains holding it all in. Jennifer and I were about to giggle our way into the giggle hall of fame. My dad woke up right at the time he always did. He walked down to the kitchen and we heard several little crashes, a couple of really big crashes, and then nothing. We came down the stairs slowly and peaked our heads around the corner. I swear to God, he looked like a bear that had just crashed a camping site. He was sitting in the middle of the kitchen with the refrigerator door broken off, food scattered and cupboard drawers in pieces. He looked at us as he was finishing off a hostess cupcake. He didn't say a word, just kept eating. Jennifer and I ran upstairs and laughed and laughed and laughed. When we woke up we heard, "God dammit girls, what happened to the kitchen??" My dad didn't remember anything.

My sister was able to read my dad much better than I did. I don't even think she even knew what she was doing, but as soon as my dad would show signs of agitation she was off to a friend's house. I on the other hand had no friends, so I was left with Bad Dad much more often. As I look back it was very cyclical, like my moods, but as a child I did not understand this. Most of the time you had a day or two of agitation before he flipped, but sometimes it was instant. I would just start to feel comfortable and I would start telling myself that maybe Bad Dad was gone and then: boom, he was back. My sister and I have even discussed in detail if he had multiple personalities. It maybe took a day or two for the agitation to build, but it took only a second for his whole demeanor to change. I don't know if we really believed the multiple personality theory or we were just trying to rationalize the irrational.

"Dad, can I go on the field trip tomorrow with Mrs. White's class?" I forget exactly where we were going or what we were going to do, but I really wanted to go. "It's twenty dollars." My dad responded, "Sure little one, I'll give you the money in the morning. Go and get me the authorization form and I'll sign it." A couple of hours went by and I was sitting in my room. "Jules, get your fucking ass down here right now!" I don't remember what my dad was mad about; all I remember is that this was a bad one. He yelled and yelled for hours, throwing stuff and finally caught me running through the house and trying to get away from him. He backed me into a corner and yelled at me with his nose almost touching mine. If I close my eyes I can still remember his face; it's haunting me to this day. I remember crying and crying, asking what I had done and all I got back was the, "bitch," "spoiled" "asshole," all the regular words. "If you think you are going on that field trip you fucking bitch you are sadly mistaken, you rotten piece of shit!" No need to go into too much detail. It's the same track record over and over again. But this time something else happened. He finally passed out and I fell asleep with my pillow over my head, only to be woken up by him at seven fifteen. "Hey little one, come on! You're running late. I've left the twenty dollars on the table; have a good field trip today." With that he left my room and was out the door. He didn't remember anything. No wonder he always acted like nothing happened. I always thought it was because he didn't want to talk about it. Was it actually because he didn't remember?

Melissa and I had only been together for a couple of months when I came home to what I thought was an empty house. I put my stuff down and walked into the bedroom, and Melissa jumped out to scare me. It's something that a lot of couples do to inject excitement into their relationship. When she did this to me that day, I fell to the ground and crawled backwards until I found a corner. I grabbed my legs, buried my head and cried for over an hour. Melissa tried to comfort me, but I was in a different place and I just told her to leave me the fuck alone. After an hour or so of crying I lifted my head to see Melissa was still there, waiting for me to ask her to hold me. She has never scared me since and understands that when you are dealing with someone who has been abused as a child, they have certain triggers. Being scared is one of mine. So don't scare me, just a little FYI in case we run into each other at the market. You got it? Right, no scary, Jules.

Jennifer was able to compartmentalize much better than me and just understood that we had two dads. She avoided Bad Dad and only tried to be around Good Dad. In our family I was supposed to be the smart one, but when it came to this, Jennifer ran circles around me. She would laugh with Dad and play jokes on him and I always thought, "Are you crazy, Jennifer? You are playing with fire!" If he started to get angry she would say something funny like, "Okay freak, I'll be back when the asshole is gone." Then she would leave for a friend's house for the night and I'm glad she did; no reason for both of us to be tormented. I was unable to do this, and I started to shut down emotionally. I just avoided my dad at all costs. It hurt his feelings, and even though this might sound strange, as I look back I feel bad for ignoring and avoiding my dad. I stopped playing sports and just went to school and up to my room. When my dad went to bed I would go downstairs and watch TV. Even though this doesn't make sense, my father worried about me terribly. He was a good man trapped by his relentless demons. I began to internalize everything, and my emotional bank began to click on low early in life.

At school I would try from time to time to make friends, but I just didn't understand kids my own age. The girls wanted to talk about the boys and the boys wanted to talk about the girls. I just wanted to talk to someone who wanted to talk about something other than girls or boys. I wanted to talk about the deeper meaning of life, and kids would look at me like I had three eyes. I would trap Jennifer in her room and make her listen to me about my feelings and life, and she would sit as long as she could and then say, "It's okay just to have fun, sis." With her newfound wisdom I would get on my bike and ride around the neighborhood and start to feel better. I would come home and my dad would be in a good mood and I would again think, "Maybe Bad Dad is gone."

Two hours or a day or two later, and Bad Dad would be back. It seemed like every time I would try and pull myself out from this pensive hole of negativity, my dad's rage would scare me back. After a couple of years of this I checked out. I mean, really checked out. I didn't talk much, if at all, and I tried to hide within the walls. I had two emotions, sad and pissed, and sometimes they came at the same time. I don't know if this was the beginning of Bipolar or the ending of what abuse caused, or both combined. All I knew at the time was that I was miserable.

I keep coming back to the fact that my sister dealt with everything so much differently than I did because she did. Maybe it has to do with her having a normal brain and me having a bipolar brain. Whatever the case, she didn't get through our childhood unscathed either. At fourteen she turned into the party girl. At first she had a lot of fun and it was a way for her to escape. I enjoyed the beginning of her partying days, too. All of her friends would come over and they were popular, cool and, my favorite part, really pretty. One benefit that I enjoyed almost daily was that when I saw them at school, they would actually say Hi to me. Jennifer always chose really nice people to be around; party girls, but kind party girls. If you look at my Facebook today, all of Jennifer's old friends from high school are all my friends on Facebook, and they still call me "little sis". In fact, I post comments about once every two weeks and I usually get one or two replies, one from my sister and one from Melissa. Today I posted a funny picture of Jennifer and me and it's like I smoked out an ant pile. I got seven posts in ten minutes. From time to time I post something of myself and Jennifer to get that feeling of being popular; I'm still such a dork.

When we were younger Dad would get us donuts on Saturdays, and all the girls who had stayed the night with Jennifer would pile down the stairs and watch cartoons with me. If I wasn't up yet they'd grab the donuts and bring them to my room, and we would all eat them together on my bed. Jennifer always included me and so did her friends, and this was really cool and something I think Jennifer knew I needed.

Jennifer had one friend named Jenny. Jenny was hilarious, and if you sprinkled a little Jennifer in the mix it was like a comedy club. "Dude, where's my mascara, dude?" Jennifer would reply, "I don't know, dude, where is your mascara, dude?" Jenny: "Dude, do I have too much mascara on?" Jennifer: "No dude, it looks good, dude." This would go on for hours until I would say, "Enough with the dude you guys." They would both look at me like I was crazy. They knew they were NOT over using the word "dude" and that I was the true dork. I found myself in the corner of my sister's room many a Friday and Saturday night watching these two "dude" out their faces. When they were done and all dolled up we would trot downstairs to watch TV.

It didn't take long until sitting with me wasn't enough for these two. Even though they were fourteen and not supposed to go out they realized that my father passed out at about 7-8pm, got up at about 9:30pm and then went down for the rest of the night. After that, nothing woke him up.

"Dude, let's sneak out dude." What in the hell were they thinking? My dad would kill them if he found out, I thought. They didn't let my fear stop them and they were gone, every Friday and Saturday night. Every Saturday and Sunday morning about 4am I'd hear, "dink, dink," on my window and I knew that was my clue to go downstairs and let them in. This went on for quite of while. Some days it would just be them, and sometimes they would let others crash over, but the crashers had to stay in the closet and leave when my dad left in the morning. It was like clockwork and I thought it was hilarious that they got away with it. Sometimes my dad would say, "Umm, I don't remember parking this close to the curb," and my eyes would get super wide because I knew he would figure it out soon. This gave me such pleasure; I didn't have to be with them to have fun. Watching them pull the wool over my dad's eyes was quite enough for me.

Jennifer was not as scared of our dad as I was. My father and Jennifer were both dyslexic and because of this I think it bonded him on a softer level with Jennifer. He felt sorry for her because he knew what it was like to grow up with dyslexia. I challenged my dad mentally; hell, I could read better than him by the age of four. I usually won the challenges, and I think this made him feel dumb. Feeling dumb made my dad angry, and since I was the one that made him feel dumb I was a target when he was raging.

"Leave her alone," I said to Renee Bunch. Renee was a bully and she was picking on some little girl for no reason. I could go into detail, but basically she was a bully. I opened my mouth to the bully, a very bipolar II thing to do. The bully then tormented me for weeks and wanted to fight me. I was tortured because I didn't want to fight. I told Jennifer about it and the day she wanted to fight me. She told me she'd take care of it and not to worry. She said, "Just show up when you are supposed to." The afternoon came. No Jennifer and one Renee Bunch walking closer to me with a pile of friends behind her. I turned to run like a screaming girl when I saw my sister and a pile of her older, prettier and more popular friends. There were about ten of them. I started to smile and turned around to face Renee Bunch. I had a surge of confidence and I believe I went too far. "You want a piece of me, you bully piece of shit?

Come on, let's go, bitch." Renee turned and walked away. I found my sister's face and I said, "I went too far, didn't I, Jennifer?" She smiled and said, "A little." She hugged me and then I piled into the back seat of my sister's Honda Prelude and she tortured me with several donuts in a dirt field until I cried a little and we went home.

Her and her friends would do donuts with her Honda Prelude in the dirt field by the school every morning. Jennifer went around and around until I would start crying and ask her to stop. Jennifer wasn't a saint by any means. God, I didn't like those donuts.

Well, Renee Bunch never bothered me again. Jenny told me several years later that they went to her house later that day after they dropped me off and talked to Renee and told her to leave me alone or she would be messing with Jennifer Alexander, not Jules Alexander anymore. Some people would have taken credit for getting someone to leave them alone, but I believe my sister knew I needed to think I had something to do with it. Jennifer and I leaned on each other far more than sisters; we also parented each other when we were able to.

To put it plainly, Jennifer was my soft place to fall as a child. That's why when Jennifer's partying turned into drug abuse it was another blow to me that was hard to take. My mother, father and sister were all alcoholic drug addicts at the time I was hitting puberty. I definitely would not recommend this. No matter how much Jennifer tried to be the life of the party, she was hurting and turned to alcohol and drugs as her own soft place to fall.

Every year my dad's grandmother, my great-grandmother would have a Christmas party. I was always so excited for these get-togethers. Everyone would go to her fabulous house that had leopard and elephant sculptures and secret hallways. It was so cool. The main thing that I liked about this was that I got to feel like I had a family for one day of the year. What I didn't realize was that the reason everyone went to this party was to get the yearly check from her. My great-grandmother was such a nice lady, she always tried to help and be kind. She knew that everyone only came around for money. No matter what she did or did not decide to do with her money, it was never right and it always caused so much pain. I'm glad I didn't realize this when I was younger, because I loved these parties.

Her house was on the side of a mountain in Miami and the driveway was a straight shot up. If you didn't have a good strong car, I bet it would not have made it up this steep driveway. All the furniture was so elegant and white; I remember a lot of white. Her pool in the backyard was decked out with mini sculptures and water features. The side of the yard that was parallel to the cliff had a huge sheet of glass. I always thought she had done that just for me, because I was such a klutz.

The parties would last about three hours, and when it came time to go I wanted to scream, "No! Not yet, grandma, not yet!" The family that I dreamed about at school was real for one day of the year, and three hours was just not enough. I wanted to tell her, "Grandma, I don't want a check, keep your money I just want to stay here with you and all my cousins and pretend no one drinks or does drugs and yells or hits. Please, take the check, take it, I don't want it! I don't care about the money, grandma." But the end would come and I would get my hundred-dollar check and get into my dad's truck and we would drive home.

One year Dad announced that we were not going to the party. It probably had to do with money that he thought he was entitled to or that a sibling or cousin had gotten that he had not gotten. My poor great-grandma! I bet she wished she never had money. But money is like good looks: if you have them, not too many would say, "Here, I don't want them, take them away." Money and looks are a revolving curse if you don't have a good foundation. I hope my great-grandma had a good foundation; she didn't deserve to be treated like she was. When my dad told us about not going to the party, my heart sank. I don't get my three hours, I thought. I know it was only three hours, but that was a lifetime to feel loved like I felt there. I was devastated to say the least.

I finally got the nerve to tell my dad that I really wanted to go, and would it be ok if Jennifer took me? He agreed and Jennifer agreed to take me, so I was back to the excited feeling. Jennifer was always running to go here and there with her friends, and every time I saw her I would say, "Don't forget about the Christmas party!" Jennifer would tell me to chill out; she remembered.

The day came and I started to get ready about four hours early to make sure I looked good for all the "family" pictures. Three hours before the party I tried to wake Jennifer up. She would not budge. Two hours, she would not budge. One hour to the party, she would not budge. I sat by her bed, telling her it was time to get up. Finally she opened her eyes. She had the same angry eyes my dad would get in a rage. I was confused. She picked me up, opened her door and threw me out, telling me to leave her the fuck alone. "Walk to the fucking party!"

Of course I cried. I was confused and hurt, and I didn't understand. Jennifer knew how important this was to me. How could she do this? Turns out that when you do crystal meth and you don't sleep for a long period of time your body will shut down if it needs to. If you wake someone up that is in this state they wake up aggressive, agitated and, at the very least, pissed. Days passed. Jennifer didn't even remember this and apologized when I told her about it. I was left thinking that I was living with the craziest motherfuckers that ever lived on the face of the planet. I was on Planet Nut-so and my father and mother were the leaders of the entire World of Nut-so. I mean, what can I say? I was devastated.

I somehow got my dad's sister's number, aunt Melody, and asked her to come and get me to take me to the party. She did. Aunt Melody was a crazy lady in her own right. She was about a size 18 to 20, but when Jennifer and I were little we used to go see her and she'd take us clothes shopping. She would browse the ranks that were size 5 and 6. She'd say, "This is going to look great on me." Jennifer and I would look at each other, and of course Jennifer would say, "Why don't you try it on for us, aunt Melody?" And then we'd giggle. To which aunt Melody would say, "I don't have to; this is going to look great." We always wondered what she did with all the clothes she bought that obviously did not fit her. Aunt Melody wore this bright white lipstick and always smelled of expensive perfume. Even though she was a bit off she was a cool lady. I didn't care if she was CRAZY AS A LOON; she was my aunt and every time I saw her I cherished it. We had the one side dimple in common. You know, the one side of your face that has a dimple and the other side of your face says, "That's all, we are going for the no-dimple look on this side."

The party came and went, but she stopped in when she dropped me off to say Hi to her brother. She stayed for an hour or so and I thought, cool, four hours of family time. She invited us to her house for Christmas. My father accepted. So the next week we were at her house, celebrating Christmas with her and her daughters. My aunt was bossy and wouldn't stop moving. She reminded me of how my mother and now my sister would act. Her hands and face would twitch and she wouldn't finish a sentence. I thought to myself, is she doing meth as well? She couldn't; she's too heavy, and heavy people are not tweakers, I thought. As soon as that thought ended, my sister nudged me to look on the side table. On the table was a huge line of white powder.

Great, now everyone is in Nut-so Land but me.

Three weeks later my father got a call from my cousin Wendy, aunt Melody's daughter. My aunt went into cardiac arrest and was in intensive care. She stayed in intensive care for six months and to this day has slurred speech and is mildly retarded. Drugs... good stuff, huh?

It was soon after that my mother got a divorce from her second husband, an abusive Italian man named Gene. Gene was an asshole and I was glad he was leaving my mom's life. My mom is like an asshole magnet. It's quite fascinating; I believe she should be studied. A lot can be learned from her. Something happens, though, when my mother does not have a man. First, she would proclaim her love for Jennifer and me. Second, she would start drinking and doing drugs. This was a pattern that was never-ending with my mother.

My mother convinced my dad to let us live with her and he agreed. My mom rented a condo in a decent neighborhood. I was thirteen at the time and about to enter high school. Once I left my dad's house and was living with my mom I started to come out of my shell; I wasn't so scared all the time anymore. My mom took me aside and told me that I was gaining a bit of weight due to puberty, and she gave me a couple of tips on how to stay thin. I thought that was so cool, my mom giving me advice. I adhered to everything she said: "No soda, only un- sweetened tea. Only eat when you are hungry and limit your sugar." I lost fifteen pounds in about four weeks, and I was so proud of myself. My mom also encouraged me to try out for soccer. I listened and made the varsity team as a freshman, which was not an easy thing to do. I thought several years off the field would really hinder me, but it didn't, and I was right back in the groove.

When high school began I was looking good, playing varsity soccer and living with my mom and Jennifer – things were great. I developed pretty large breasts over the summer and kept my tiny waist. I looked like a Florida girl with the long blonde hair, and I caught the eye of quite a few guys in the upper grades. I can still remember: "Jules, Tom is here to see you. You fucking bitch, sis, I've had a crush on him for three years!" Jennifer was jealous of my newfound attention, but she was happy for me.

What she didn't understand was that I did not seem to care one bit about boys; they did absolutely nothing for me. I would kind of be interested from a challenge point, but as soon as they reciprocated a desire I was gone like the wind. This in turn caused them to fight harder and made me a target for all the popular hot guys in school. It's safe to say that no boy caught me, though. I'd go out on dates, but as soon as something physical would happen, I would run like the wind.

We all lived in this condo for about three months before the shit hit the fan. One night at about 11pm I was alone at home on the couch. Suddenly the front door flew open and I jumped off the couch in fright. It was my sister. She was on her knees and looking all around. "They know, they fucking know." I replied, "They know what, Jennifer?" "They know I know, and they're after me!" Jennifer looked like a crazy woman walking on her knees to the window, looking out to make sure "they" were not there. Apparently Jennifer had ingested some hallucinogen. We were up the entire night. I started to play the game to soothe her. "Jennifer, there's no one out there. You got away, sis." She looked around, trying to believe me. "Are you sure, Jules?" "Yep, I'm sure." After a four-hour marathon of this she finally went to bed. My mother didn't come home that night until about five in the morning, so she missed all the fun, but I wouldn't dare tell on Jennifer. Her secret was safe with me.

After that night I said, Fuck it. If everyone in my entire family is doing drugs, I'm going to sign up. I talked my sister into letting me try crystal meth and she agreed. Yuck! The stuff tasted awful going down, but within minutes I felt this euphoria. Jennifer and Jenny were getting ready to go out and I begged them to let me go. They agreed and I went to the bathroom to curl my hair. When I came out they were gone. I knew that they would probably be right back and my hair wasn't perfect, so I decided to wash it and start over. I did this about three times until I realized that my sister was not coming back. I spent the remainder of the night cleaning and re-curling my fried hair. I was so pissed, but I believe my sister felt bad for letting me try it.

After that night I begged Jennifer to let me go out with her and she refused. In fact, she told everybody at our high school to not party with her sister. I was off limits! Jennifer told me after we became adults that she knew I wouldn't have been strong enough to pull myself out. So she put an invisible guard around me and no one dared to cross Jennifer. She was too popular and everyone wanted her to like them.

I was still determined to become a partier though. My mother started staying out all night, tweaking with all her friends, and Jennifer was out tweaking with all her friends. I was left alone. I used my big breasts, long blonde hair, bright green eyes and big lips to get a couple of older guys from another high school take me out. I didn't tell Jennifer and I just snuck out. That's funny to say that I snuck out on my sister. My mother was gone all the time doing drugs, so I didn't need to sneak out on her, she was gone baby gone.

The guys picked me up in a lifted blue truck and I thought I was cool. In retrospect I can say, how dumb was I? We started drinking wine coolers and went to a party. I remember smoking pot. After that it fades in and out. They took me to a mountain of some kind and they raped me. The memory is fuzzy, very fuzzy, but I woke up the next morning and my vagina was on fire, so I'm pretty sure they raped me. Thank God I don't remember most of the details. I've often wondered if my soul does. To which I answer myself yes, probably.

"Get back here you son of a bitch," my sister yelled. My head bobbled on the front lawn as my sister ran past me to catch the two boys that had thrown me on the grass. Jennifer came back and picked me up. She put my arm around her neck and took me to the bathroom to wash the puke out of my hair. She started to cry. "Jules, God dammit, you are too smart for this. Don't do this to yourself!" She yelled and cried at me for what seemed like hours.

She undressed me, put me in the bathtub and got in behind me to hold me up. She washed me, crying and begging me not to do this again. Even though this is still fuzzy to me, she made her point and I never became a party girl.

When I woke up that morning I went to run into my mother's room; I needed her. I was thirteen and I needed my mom. The room was empty; she hadn't come home that night. I went downstairs to find Jennifer at the kitchen table. She asked me what had happened. I never told her the truth. I just told her I got drunk and ended the conversation. I don't think she believed me, but she was only sixteen and not able to figure out what to do either. That was our mother's job, but she was too busy banging guys and doing drugs to be bothered with her daughters.

It seemed like only weeks had passed and our mother was only home a day or two out of the week. The cupboards became bare and we were hungry. My sister called our dad and he came and got us. I was devastated.

After this my sister really dove off the deep end with drugs. I gave up and went back into my shell. I started obsessively listening to The Judds. I wanted Naomi to be my mother and I fantasized about it to an unhealthy level. I even went so far as to buy clothes and tailor them to what I thought Wynonna would wear. I would go up to my room and listen to their music and sing into my hairspray can and just pretend. I decided that I was going to be a country music singer, and this fantasy got me through the next year or so. The only problem with the singer solution was that I CANNOT sing. It's not like I can sing a little and just needed to practice. I could not and still cannot carry a tune in a bucket. I got a part-time job to pay for guitar lessons and singing lessons, and I went to every session for about a year. One day, though, the singing coach talked to me about this fantasy. I believe she let me continue for so long because she knew I needed it. My singing coach was a nice woman and would really listen to me, and I looked forward to the conversations. I would try to avoid singing because no matter how hard I tried it was awful, really bad. "Jules, honey... I don't think this is for you, sweetie," she said, "you can come here anytime and talk if you like, but I feel like I'm just taking your money." I agreed and never went back.

After my teenage dream was shattered, I gave up and sunk into a deep depression. This was the time my father brought home the puppy that was supposed to cure me. I cried every day and that was it. I cried every day. My grades fell below average and I just gazed in my classes. If I was asked a question I just shrugged my shoulders.

"Mom, please help me, please. I can't live with Dad, I'm scared," I cried into the phone. She came and got me. She knew that she was not in a place to care for me, so she called her parents in Washington. She asked her mother to let me live with them. My grandmother refused and said, "I'm tired of raising kids." She had raised my aunt Sarah's kids most of their lives, and she quite frankly didn't enjoy raising kids.

My grandfather, on the other hand, loved kids. I used to go up to their farm some summers and Granddad and me had a blast. He would always tell me how smart I was and how proud he was of me. He's taken me places and we didn't have to talk; I just knew he loved me. I was his little shadow. When the time would end and I had to go home I just didn't want it to end. Even though my grandma was kind of a bitch, she still was okay, and my granddad was my angel. He was the kind of guy who would say, "If you mow the lawn I'll give you half a dollar," and when you finished he'd inspect it and say, "Good job." He'd pull out the dollar and tear it in half and say, "Here you are." I loved my granddad. He was so stable and he would be the same granddad everyday all day and I was his favorite. He encouraged me and loved me and encouraged me and loved me over and over again. So when my grandma refused to let me live with them it was just another blow, and my mom took me back to my dad's house in her funky bright yellow Ford Ranger.

My sixteenth birthday came and my dad bought me a new car, woohoo. He also bought a new fancy house, too; he had received his inheritance on his 40th birthday. Jennifer had moved to Washington to live with my grandparents. Jennifer had become a total drug addict and needed to go somewhere she could be away from all her old acquaintances. I missed her terribly, but was ready to start my senior year and move out.

"Jules, come here," my tennis coach summoned. I had tried out and made the varsity tennis team, and I was excited and recharged for my senior year. "Do you know that your grade point average fell below 2.0 last semester?" I knew it had, but I thought no one would catch it. "Jules, if your grade point average falls below 2.0 you can't play sports. I'm sorry, but you can't practice anymore. You need to go home."

I came in the door and thought I should tell my dad; he would have found out sooner or later, so I did: "Dad, I can't play tennis. My grade point average fell below 2.0." My dad flipped. I have no idea why; I never knew when or why he would flip. He went into his normal rants and it escalated to physical. I turned to run down the hall and he pushed me to the floor. I crawled as fast as I could to get away from him and ran to my car. I ripped open the door and put it into gear fast enough that my father didn't catch me. I had it, I had it.

I was done. Do you get the drift? Done, done, done. I didn't know what I was going to do, but I knew I was not going back to that house again. I missed my sister and I didn't want to be my dad's rage collector any longer. I had collected enough rage for 50 in my short lifetime. I felt a surge of confidence. I thought about going to a shelter, living on the streets. I thought I would start by calling my grandparents and try one more time. I called from this stinking hot phone booth wiping my tears and trying to hold in my body trembles. "Hello." It was my granddad. I blurted out in-between my sobs, "I know you guys don't want to raise another kid, but I'm sixteen and I can take care of myself. I just want a bed to sleep on. Please Granddad, let me live with you guys. Just for a little bit until I can figure out what to do next." I went on for probably five or six minutes, just ranting and raving to which he replied, "Of course you can, why would you think you could not live with us?" "Grandma said she was tired of raising kids when me and Mom called two years ago." Silence. "She what? Listen: you can come live with us. I will deal with your grandma. Do you need money? I will send you money, where are you at?"

While I was hanging up the phone I heard my granddad say, "Dammit woman, come here! We need to talk." I had the biggest smile on my face. My knight and shining armor was my granddad and he was the first angel in my life. I would have many more, but he was my first. When I let myself go back to this day and what my granddad did for me it brings tears of joy that I can't control. It's like I'm sixteen all over again.

I had to go back to my house to get my clothes and things. My mind raced on about how I was going to get past my dad. I returned to the house, quietly walked into my room and started throwing things into a dark plastic bag. My father entered my room and asked me what I was doing. "Dad, I don't want to live here any longer. Granddad says I can live with them for my last year of high school. I miss Jennifer and I just want to leave." He turned from the doorway and as he did he muttered, "Okay."

After I was packed I threw my bags into the car and started on my journey to Tacoma, Washington.

Chapter 6
Last Year of High School

"So Jules, what kind of grades were you getting at your old school? You know, I don't accept anything less than a B in this house, especially as smart as you are," My granddad spouted while we were on our way to sign me up for my new high school. I just wanted him to be proud of me, so when the counselor asked me the same questions about grades and classes I replied, "I'm in all honor classes and I get straight As."

Holy shit, what was I thinking? I hadn't gotten an A in anything but physical education in years. When the counselor called me into her office six weeks later to inform me that she had received my transcript and was surprised to see my grades. I immediately said, "Yes but I'm in honors classes now, and I'm getting straight As. Can't I just stay?" I didn't want my granddad to be disappointed.

He wasn't. After my counselor spoke with my teachers she was, as she put it, "pleasantly surprised" with the extraordinary job I was doing and let me stay in all my classes.

For the first time in my academic career I had peace, constant peace in my home. My grandparents lived on a farm in Tacoma, Washington, and it was beautiful. Every morning I would wake up in the most comfortable bed I had ever slept in. I'd get myself ready knowing that no one was going to flip out or be on drugs. I would leave the house every day with my granddad saying, "Do your best, because your best is great." Sometimes after I heard that I would tear up on my way to school because I was so happy and thankful. All I needed was to have someone believe in me with consistency. My father would believe in me one day and compare me to shit the next. My Grandfather was exactly what I needed at the exact time I needed him.

Because I was in some honors classes I met the honors kind of kids. These kids did the right things and not one of them did drugs. I was amazed and I felt like I could finally breathe. One of the girls, Megan, was on the soccer team. I started two weeks into the school year, so the soccer team was practicing and getting ready for their first game. I tried out and made the team. In fact, I was the best on the team. This school was quite a bit smaller than my old school in Miami and it wasn't that big of an accomplishment to be the best on the team, but I ate it up. I tried as hard as my little legs would let me.

My granddad came to my first game and cheered me on. On the way home he asked me, "Jules, what college are you going to go to when you finish high school? You know, I bet you could get a soccer scholarship." Up until that moment I had not really even thought about it. I was always too busy just trying to survive; I never thought I could go to college. My wheels began to turn. I hung out with a group of the straightest friends in the entire universe – or that's what it felt like coming from what I came from. No one did drugs; no one had sex; they all had moms and dads who were calm and comforting. I never told them what I came from; I didn't want them to think I was weird. These were the Christian kids in school. I had never given God a thought other than when I was praying for him not to let me hear my mom have sex with some strange guy. Or when I was pleading, asking God to make my mom come home and not do drugs or drink. I pleaded to God asking that he take my dad's rage away. God never came through, for me so I wasn't a big fan to say the least. I was skeptical of this "God" thing, but all these kids and parents seemed so joyful and honest and clean, like they had just been put through a car wash. It was strange to me to say the least, but I liked it. After a while I began to pray. I started to understand that "God" can't help people who don't want to be helped or don't do anything to change. I also started to understand that I was starting to become an adult and I could make my own choices. I wanted to be like these kids and these families. I was happy for the first time that I can remember in my entire childhood.

One day we were on the way to a soccer match when our coach spoke up. "I have a letter here from a soccer coach from a private college in the Midwest. They are starting a girls' soccer program. If any of you girls are interested in playing soccer on a college soccer scholarship, come and see me." Holy shit, I thought, God is listening to me and opening up doors for me. I desperately wanted to go to college, but my father wasn't going to pay for it and my mother was definitely not able to help. I jumped up and almost hit my head on the roof of the bus. "Me! Me! Me, coach, me, me, I'd like to go! I'd like to play! I wanna go, can I go, pick me! Please, please, please?" The roar of the girls on the bus was embarrassing. I was starting to realize, being around these "normal" people, that I didn't really know how to act or be. But I didn't care; my drive to succeed was starting to kick in and I was going to be successful no matter what.

I ran to the house and just about busted down the door. Grandma dropped a pan she was carrying to the sink. "Granddad, Granddad!" I yelled, "Look, look! They are looking for soccer players and I could get a scholarship!"

He read the letter. "This is great, Jules. You can do this." We sat down at the kitchen table and discussed what to do next. Are you fucking kidding me? I had an adult who loved me and who was discussing how I could get a goal accomplished. What fucking planet was I on, because I wanted to stay on this planet.

They were asking us to submit a video of a soccer game I had played in and mail it ASAP. Granddad ran to the closet and got the video camera. The next week he came to my soccer game and videotaped the whole thing. He took me to the post office and helped me package it and send it off. This simple act was huge for me. I had an adult who, number one, believed it me consistently and, number two, helped me work to my goals and, number three, loved me consistently. I was thankful.

It took only weeks to get the reply, but you could have marooned me on an island for seven years and it would have felt like the same. I can still remember that day and what it felt like opening the front door and seeing my granddad at the dinner table, drinking tea. "Jules, look!"

He was looking at this letter like he was going to magically see into it. My grandfather seemed as nervous as I was. I started to open the letter and my grandma came into the kitchen to offer support. "Dear Jules, we would like to offer you—"

With that much of the letter read it was enough to send me running through the house skipping like I was four years old. When I finally returned I realized they were offering me a partial scholarship. Partial? Who cares! It was somebody else saying they believed in me.

The following week I spoke to the counselor and realized this was a very expensive school. This was a private college and it cost more than a pretty penny. I felt the wind starting to fade under my wings, but my granddad wouldn't let that happen. "Jules, we'll apply for scholarships. You can do this." What he didn't know was that I wasn't a straight A student who took honors classes. The next day I talked with the school counselor and found a "turn-around scholarship." This scholarship was for a student like me, one who started below average but finished above average. My counselor and I agreed that this would be a good one for me to apply for. But even with this scholarship and the soccer scholarship I still wasn't half way there, and I didn't even realize I needed room and board.

I returned home from school with realizing this was just not going to happen and I was just acquiescing with the idea. I casually told my granddad that I had realized I would not be able to go to college. He put his hands on my shoulders and knelt down to make sure I was looking in his eyes. "Jules, life doesn't drop opportunities in your lap. You have to find them and then convince the opportunities that you are the one." He asked me if I understood. I nodded, but I didn't really. I was still beaten down and unable to think my way out of the situation. I think my granddad understood that even though I told him what he wanted to hear.

When I came home from school the following day I was surprised to find my granddad in his office. He asked me to come in. My granddad looked so smart to me. He sold cars successfully for over 20 years and then opened a motorcycle dealership. In his retirement he had started a real estate company and had a little mom and pop dog and cat boarding business. To me he was a genius and I looked up to him. After I sat down in front of his desk he looked up and said, "Jules, do you know that I can't read or write well? Do you know that your grandmother has always had to help me with reading and writing? Did you also know that I ran away from home as a boy and whatever I set out to do, I did? I never let anyone tell me that I couldn't do anything, because I knew I could. You can figure this out. We can figure this out together. What you can't do is quit at something before you even start to try. If you do, you are like all the other average people in this world. I'm going to help you figure this out, so in the future you can see that things can be figured out. You just have to keep on until you get what you want."

After dinner my grandparents and I talked about how I could get the rest of the money. My granddad asked me about my great-grandmother, my father's grandmother. My great- grandmother was the heir in my great-grandfather's estate and was worth quite a bit of money. I put a caboose on that idea, telling them that my father would kill me if I asked her for money. My father always told me that he never took any money from her, that he would never ask her for money, and that he would just kill me if I did. "Your father is full of shit, Jules. He asked her for money all the time, just like all the other grandkids." I was taken aback by this. I had heard the constant ranting about how all his siblings and cousins lived off my great-grandmother and he never asked for a dime. I didn't know if my granddad was telling me the truth or my father. However my granddad convinced me that I was standing for something that would cut my knees off and inhibit me from being successful. Successful was something that was always in the back of my mind. The word and all that it encompassed – successful. While living with my father I had stopped trying to be successful because I felt beaten down. Now that I was away from him and with my granddad I wanted this word back in my life.

I sat down that evening and started to write a letter to my great-grandma:

"Dear Great-Grandma,

I'm sorry to have to write this to you. I know that it seems like everyone comes to you for money and I am just another in a long line. But I'm about halfway through my senior year in high school and I would like to go to college. I can't get a grant because my father has too much money from his inheritance, and he doesn't want to pay for my college. I think he is scared that he is going to run out of money. He hasn't worked in years and I think he thinks he can't.

I have been accepted to a private college in the Midwest. I got a soccer scholarship that covers about 1/4 of the tuition, but I don't have the rest and room and board.

Grandma, I don't want to be a loser and I'm trying to be successful, but it seems like no one wants me to be. I just need help and I promise I will do everything I can to make you and the Alexander name proud.

Sincerely,
Jules Alexander"

When I dropped that letter off before school I was excited. At lunch I got a major panic attack because I knew this would beyond piss my father off if he know about it. Even though I was not living with my father, his rage still lived inside me and I was terrified. I raced back to my grandparents' house and prayed that they didn't see me at the end of the driveway. I pulled the lever on the mailbox. The letter was gone. I was excited and terrified at the same time. "Holy shit!" I thought. I was excited that I didn't catch it, but devastated as well. I went back to school and got there just in time for my next class.

This period was an "office assistant" class. I helped the admin with paperwork. Her name was Terry and she was one of many people that I believe God placed in front of me to learn and get love from. I opened up to her about my life. She asked me questions about my life and had a sincerity to learn about me. After a couple of months she knew more than most people in my life. She felt safe. Every time I came into the office she would give me a big hug and say, "There is my future successful woman!" This was my favorite moment of the day. Terry was a mother to two boys who were in college, and she boasted about them and was so proud. She baked them cookies and sent them to them regularly. She talked about their trials and tribulations with girls' situations and school and decisions, like where to get a job and whether to drop a class or stick it out. She was everything that I had fantasized about as a child. If I was to design a mother, Terri is what I would have made.

Terry knew that I was going to mail the letter that morning, and she didn't forget. "There is my future successful woman!" She held on a little longer than usual and she said, "Did you do it? I know you did, how are you?" When she let go she saw me crying. I felt so bad about doing this to my father, and I said so to Terry. She sat me down and pulled a chair next to me. "I want you to really listen to what I'm going to say to you. Are you really listening?" I nodded.

She grabbed a tissue and wiped my tears for me, as a mother would. "Jules, you are a super special girl. I have had hundreds of office assistants and you are the only one who has stood out for me. Life has dealt you a real terrible hand. Most of the kids I have in here have parents who are loving and kind and do everything they can to help their kids succeed, and you have the opposite. But, you try harder than all the kids I have seen combined. Fuck your father; you are doing the right thing. This is your life. Don't be trapped by the guilt and torment that he has caused, don't get into the cycle of abuse. He might be a good man, like you say, but I say let him prove it and until he does, fuck him. You did the right thing."

I was taken aback by her use of the word "fuck". She caught me off guard, and I think she was trying to. I stopped crying and we went to work. "Jules I made you some of your favorite cookies, they are in the break room. Go get a couple and get to work." I did exactly what she said and I felt better.

My father and I started to talk again while I was living with my grandparents. He was nice to talk to when I was able to get away when I needed to. My father knew I was trying to go to college and asked me if I was going to move back in with him to go to a community college. I don't think he ever quite understood how abusive he was. When you are the abuser you don't realize the impact of your actions; they are filtered down within the abuser's mind. Most abusers are not Satan worshippers and are generally good people who are unable to control their behavior. This is why so many women stay with abusers. On the inside the abusers are good people, and the abused keep praying that things will change. After an episode, as I call them, they are normal and loving, so it's fucking confusing. But just as I believe most drug addicts or alcoholics have some sort of mental illness, I believe the same for abusers. But at what point do you say that it's enough? When he would bring up the college question I would try and avoid it.

It was a short time when I received a phone call from Laurie, my father's first cousin on his father's side. She was an extremely intelligent woman. I say that in my family you are either a genius or a derelict. She was probably pretty close to the genius side. She took all the money that she received from the Alexander family and invested it and did very well for herself. She also was one of the only grandkids out of the five that took the time to make sure my great- grandma was taken care of. My great-grandma was in a fancy retirement home in Miami and Laurie took care of her and her estate. She did this out of love, but the rest of the family always thought she was greedy and money hungry. With the years that I have spent talking with her I know she is the opposite. She is a good woman, just as my great-grandmother was.

"Hi Jules, it's Laurie." My heart dropped. My father vehemently hated this woman with a passion. My father always told me that she was evil and just after money. If my father knew I was even talking to her he would skin me up on a tree. "Hi Laurie," I said. "Grandma wanted me to give you a call. She got your letter and wanted me to talk with you. She understands that you want to go to college and she wants to help, but she also wants to make sure you understand what that means." My heart sank a little further. At the same time I had a jolt of excitement knowing that she wanted to help, but I knew where she was going. "If she helps you, she has to create a trust fund to help all the great-grandkids go to college, and this will be family knowledge. She cannot just help you; she said it's not right, no matter how much she wants to. Plus, it means that she will have fewer funds to give in her inheritance to the grandkids, and this will cause real tension within the family. Also, she knows your father has such hate in his heart toward your great-grandma that if she does help she's worried about the repercussion on you. She can take it and is willing to help you be successful, but she wants you to think about it before she goes further."

My head lowered. I knew this, but when it was knowledge of someone else it had a burdening effect. "Jules, I've known you since you were a little girl and I know you have a special quality. You deserve to be successful. You do not deserve to have to deal with all you have had to, and I'm sorry. I know this is just one more thing, but it cannot be avoided. Think about it and talk with your grandparents. Let me know what you decide." I hung up the phone.
When I was still living with my dad I walked by his room one night and saw a shotgun in his hands. I asked him what he was doing with it and he said, "Cleaning it, so I can go human hunting in Oregon." I knew Laurie had just moved to Oregon so I knew what he meant by it. His eyes were the Bad Dad, so I ran to my room hoping I wasn't going to be on his human hunting list. This was the hate that my father had in his heart for Laurie; so talking to her was like talking to Satan. This was a big deal.
After I got off the phone my granddad chimed in with his thoughts. "Jules, this is your chance! Take it." I wanted to; I really did. Abusive people have such a hold on their abused and I was no different. My granddad was saying the right things and I still was unable to commit. How would my father not find out? How would I explain how I got to go to such a expensive school? My life seems to be a series of pretending to be something I'm not, and this was no different.
I called Laurie back the next night and asked her if my father was in contact with great- grandma or anyone else in the family that she

knew about. She said no. My father had written off just about everyone in his life, including his family. I thought that if he didn't talk to anyone I was safe. "I want to do it Laurie. I thought about it and I want to go to college."

"Hey Dad, it's Jules. You know that school that is interested in me for soccer? They just offered me a full ride scholarship. Cool, huh, Dad?" My dad was so proud of me. He kept saying, "Little one, I knew it. That's my girl," and all the other stuff a parent would say if they were really proud of their child. If you have ever been in an abusive relationship you understand that going against the abuser on this level takes the balls of an elephant. I had those balls that night.

Chapter 7
College

I graduated from high school and got a job at the local Godfather's Pizza. I had to save up money for my trip across country to college. I worked the regular 40 hours a week and would get a call at least once a week from my grandma: "Jules, can you make me one of those special pizzas and bring it home from work with you?" One of the only times you heard my grandma have pleasure in her voice was when it had to do with food or when she thought you looked pretty. If you had food and you looked pretty at the same time she went into happy convulsions and the paramedics would have to be called. Just kidding – we never had to call the paramedics, but it was close a couple of times. I did have a tendency to look damn good carrying a pizza.

My new soccer coach from college sent out a workout schedule that he wanted me to follow, but with working as much as I was I didn't have time. Or shall I say: I didn't make time. Spending a couple of months in a pizza shop and not working out left me with an extra fifteen pounds. Fifteen pounds on a small frame added up to a lot of extra weight. Because I had such a curvy figure it ended up in my breast and hips. Not good places for a soccer player. Most soccer players are slim and shapeless and by the end of the summer I was the opposite.

I don't think I understood how much competition I would encounter in college soccer. I thought my natural ability would shine through as it always had. I never had private coaches in soccer or much attention paid to me regarding sports. Sports got me out of the house when I was younger and got me attention that I craved. But I never had to worry about being the best; as soon as I hit the field it would usually be obvious within minutes. I could stop for a couple of years and still be the best.

When the time came I packed my car and said my goodbyes to my grandparents. I remember looking in the rear view mirror bawling; I didn't want to leave. I should not have left; I was too young and damaged to navigate through life yet. I was seventeen and I was going across the country to go to college, where I knew not a soul. I had lied to my father on how I got to college and it was a heavy burden to bear.

I had to be to school several weeks before the others because soccer players had to start training. I drove my way to Missouri and I found motels that allowed me to check in without an ID. I drove into the little town where the college was located. I kept waiting for the city to appear. It was so small and, being from Miami, I wasn't used to small. When I arrived I found my dorm room and took my box from my car and unpacked it in a matter of minutes. I didn't know what to do, so I went to bed at six and tried to sleep. I was too excited, though: practice was a 5am the next morning. I was pumped.

"Girls! Line up, we are going to do sprints." Fuck, I was terrible at sprints. I was not as fast as soccer players usually are, and I knew this was not going to be a good start. I ran as fast as my little legs and breasts would let me and I came in last. Having double-D breasts made running even that much harder. I thought to myself, "If these bitches had double-Ds they'd be a lot slower, too." I chuckled to myself trying to support my ego. The rest of the day was running, mixed in with more running and topped off with a little more running. These girls had listened to the coach when he sent out his requests for summer exercise.

"So what did you do this summer?" One girl asked another. "Oh, we went to our beach house and my parents hired me a personal trainer. We used the beach as our workout area. Let me tell you, the trainer was HOT!" The other: "Oh my god, my parents sent me to soccer camp in Arizona." Other: "Really, my parents were thinking about that too! How did you like it?" This went on for several minutes and most of the other girls joined in the conversation. I didn't fit in, but what's new, I thought. This was a prestigious college and it was obvious with this chatter back and forth. Fitting in was never something I did, so I just let in roll off my back. What's new, I would tell myself; just makes me stronger.

As the days turned into weeks I realized that these girls were far superior soccer players than me. I started to feel stupid and wasteful of time. I had never experienced this before and I tried to navigate through my emotions. I was at another level, a level that took every year from four on in soccer programs, private coaches, rooting parents, pats on the back, "let's figure this out"-talks with parents, and so on and so forth. I was not involved in any of these private privileges. I only had me, and that wasn't enough at this level. I pulled my coach aside and tried to tell him that I would do anything he suggested to make myself as good as these girls. I don't think he heard me when I was talking to him; he looked over me the whole time and just said, "Sure, whatever Jules." I should have flashed him the double-Ds, I thought to myself as I left with my tail between my legs. He would have noticed me then, I guarantee it.

The weeks passed and kids and parents were starting to arrive. I was excited to meet my roommate. I looked out my window and saw all the nice cars and nice looking kids with nice looking parents. I started to look for any single kids with no parents arriving. I looked for three days, and I didn't see one. What is wrong with me, I thought. But I knew. I didn't want my dad to come because I was afraid he would flip out and make a scene. My mother would be another embarrassment and I would just be terrified that she would get drunk and seduce one of the dads. "Hello, my name is Jules and here are my parents. This is David. Watch out, he could flip out at any moment and kick the shit out of you. And this is my mother; watch out for your drugs and husbands. Where do I put my stuff?"

It was the last day of arrivals and I wondered if my roommate was going to make it. She did. Her name was Carol and she had the normal parents and all the stuff to decorate her side of the room as all the other girls did. She seemed nice, and once they were all done they headed out to grab some dinner. "Hey Jules, you want to come with us?" I smiled and said if I didn't intrude I'd like to come. Her parents took us to Pizza Hut and I started to think that things were going to pick up for me.

The following couple of weeks I spent going to class and soccer practices and then coming back to my room to cry. I wasn't the best on the team; I was more like the worst. I just did not know how to deal with this and the stress of college. I came home after practice one afternoon and slammed the door and threw my cleats, sat down on my bed and screamed and then cried. I didn't realize Carol was in the room until later. I apologized and told her that soccer was not going well.

The next afternoon I came into our room and all of Carol's things were gone. In these dorm rooms you had two dorms connected by one bathroom. Our neighbor was this rich stuck up girl who was always a bitch to me. When I sat my stuff down I heard giggles across the bathroom. I opened it up to find Carol and the girl from the other side saying, "See, she's so weird." Carol had moved in with the rich girl across the bathroom.

It was starting to seem to me like my life was just going to suck. No matter how hard I tried to make it better, it always backslid the wrong way. Usually people follow in their parents' footsteps, or along the same lines. If your parents are doctors and lawyers they usually have doctor and lawyer kids. Blue-collar parents usually have blue-collar kids. This usually follows the same rules with drugs and drinking. Parents who are drug addicts and alcoholics usually produce the same. Most people just get on at the same level their parents are at because it feels comfortable. I did not want to be my parents; I wanted to be better, happier, healthy and more successful. Even though I had an extremely successful great-grandfather it was far back enough that the only benefit that came of it was that my college was paid for. I didn't want to be like my parents. I wanted to break the mold. I was intent on doing well in college, I understood the importance and the blessing I was given.

With all of that lovely stuff said. the fact is that breaking out of the tracks your parents left is hard. Why do you think we have such an obsession with Oprah Winfrey? She breaks the mold of her upbringing and she is a one-in-a-billion person. She probably slid back many times with her childhood, but she did it. I wanted to do it as well.

Soccer was miserable for the entire time I played. I actually believe I played about nine minutes in total for my freshman soccer season. My coach put me in for about five minutes to yell at the center forward, just long enough that I scored a goal. As soon as that ball went into the net I knew things were going to turn around. The other center forward had had twenty minutes and did nothing. I was given five minutes and shot one in. He didn't even let me set up for the kick off after the goal. He called me out and continued to yell at the starting center fielder as she ran on the field to take her position back. He didn't even say, "Good goal, Jules, we needed it." Nothing. This guy was a slime ball and if I had to guess, my guess would be he never amounted to anything in the coaching field. You coach for others, not for yourself. This is another in a long line of people I would love to have conversation with as my adult self. I'd like to see this fucker treat me the way he did as a grown woman.

The other four minutes were at the last game of the season. We were losing so badly (what a surprise with ass wipe as our coach) and I kept bugging him for the entire season to play that he let me in the last ten minutes of the game. I did the same thing I had done several months ago when I broke my leg. The goalie and I were running for the ball and I didn't give up, just like I hadn't several months ago. I landed on the ground, crying in agony. The coach didn't even come on the field to check on me. I hobbled my way off the field and put myself on the bench. He never asked me if I wanted to go to the doctor, or if I was okay. I couldn't walk without assistance for weeks. I didn't have insurance and I didn't have a coach who cared if I lived or died, so I let it heal on its own. To this day I don't know what I did. I just know my knee has never been the same since.

After soccer ended I focused on school. I didn't have friends, so the weekdays were okay because I kept busy, but the weekends were miserable. Before I got a job I would drive for hours upon hours in my little beige Mitsubishi. I would blare The Judds music and pretend I was Wynonna, and I would just let it rip. My college was far enough out of any big city that I could find these country roads all to myself and just wail up a storm. Let me tell you, I was a damn good singer when you couldn't hear my voice over the music. But some days I would drive with no music and just cry. These cries were pitiful. Some days it was all I could do not to pull over the side of the road and puke. These cries were raw and not normal, cries one should ever have. I wish I could go back as an adult and stop that little girl, reach out to her and say, "Hold on Jules, it gets better. Hold on honey." I bet I drove on average fifteen hours a week, crying, singing and thinking.

I befriended a girl named Melanie, who was also a freshman. She was a cute little blonde who had a limp to her when she walked. She had had some severe injury that made walking a bit of a challenge. I would go to her dorm room and we would talk for hours. She had a boyfriend back in Kansas City who she would talk about constantly. I never understood the boy thing, but I knew it was important to her, so I listened. Melanie had recently started having sex with her boyfriend and this was a hot topic with us. She would tell me about positions and places, and I was interested in hearing about it. This was new to me, because I was never interested in hearing about sex. I heard enough of my mom doing it when I was a child that it usually sickened me just by the discussion of it. But I was getting older and hormones were kicking in.

One day I decided that I wanted to have sex. I had thought I wanted to wait for a special man, but I never seemed to be interested in any men. So I went with a more strategic plan. I was probably practicing my elaborate outlines to come for strategic sales. This outline was short and to the point:

Sex
1. Go to a bar
2. Find a nice looking guy
3. Ask him if he wants to have sex

This outline was a huge success and it was completed in one weekend with a man named Gerald. Gerald was a frequent flyer at a country bar that had a huge dance floor. He was a great dancer and as soon as I saw him I said, "Yep, that's him." Guys are so easy; they really are. I sometimes think I was fucked in more ways than one with my sexuality. 1) it's so hard to be okay with your sexuality in our puritan land. 2) equality is not equal among same sex couples. 3) God and gay has a way of fucking with you even though I believe most "Christians" wouldn't know God or Christ if they showed up at their door, because they are so far from what they stand for. 4) Guys are really easy to manipulate. My goodness, how easy you have it as a straight woman, if you only knew!

That was a bit of a run on. But what I mean is that guys are EASY in so many ways.

Sex with Gerald was fun. I told him I was a virgin, because for all intents and purposes I did feel like a virgin. I had not said yes to sex with a boy or man. It was taken, so for me I felt like a virgin.

The first time we had sex Gerald realized that I was not a virgin and said something to that fact. I ignored him and he let it slide. I learned many cool things with Gerald. I learned about erect penises and cum. I have to say I never knew anything about this, so it was all a shocker to me. I never had anyone talk to me about this kind of stuff. Gerald was a good little teacher, and we had a good time having sex for a couple of months. From the beginning I never had a problem with sex. It was fun and I enjoyed it. I was never the one hidden under the blankets asking my partner turn off the lights. The second time around I had Gerald pinned down and I ran the show. I enjoyed sex. I always have.

One added benefit to Gerald was that he taught me how to dance. There is something to be said about a person who can really dance. When you dance with a leader who knows how to dance you just feel safe and cared for and everyone else can see the same thing you feel. Gerald was not bad on all levels; we had fun.

As my freshman year came to a close I decided I did not want to return for another year at the "I'm better than you"-school. I was in a real nice spot: I could go anywhere I wanted to go. I did some research and found a university near Nashville. This school had an audio engineering program that caught my eye. I have always loved and enjoyed music, so I thought this would be a perfect major for me.

Chapter 8
Falling in Love

When I went home after my freshman year I was excited to go back to Tacoma. Even though I had only lived there for a year it seemed like home to me. My dad wanted me to come to Miami for the summer, but a phone call was all I wanted to chance with my dad. That way if he started to rage I could just hang up the phone. After I had settled in my granddad pulled me aside and said, "Jules, you are still so young. Most kids your age are either going into their senior year in high school or just graduated. I know last year was hard for you. How about we go down to the community college and sign you up and you can stay here for a couple of years." I had a smile from ear to ear. Wow, how cool would that be! My excitement didn't last long because right after that my grandma pulled me aside and said, "Jules, I'm tired of raising kids and paying for my kids' kids. You will not stay with us and you will find another way through college. Is that understood?" I understood.

I decided that I would transfer to university near Nashville. In the back of my mind I still wanted to be a singer, but I would settle for their Audio Engineering program instead. This university had an extensive program for music engineers, managers, agents or anything you wanted to do in the entertainment industry. I found a summer program for Audio Engineering in Ohio and left my grandparents' house two weeks later. I told my granddad that this was super exciting and I thanked him for his offer, but said I wanted to go. My trust fund paid for tuition, room and board and food, so since my grandma wanted me out I just had to find a place to go to school for the summer and I would have my room and board paid for.

Summer ended and time came for me to drive to Nashville. When I turned on the street that the college was on, my eyes popped! The college was just huge; it looked like a city rather than a college. Cars were everywhere and there were parents and kids moving stuff in. I only had a box and myself, but I was jazzed to be there anyway. I found my dorm and unpacked. I was ready for my new adventure.

My fog was starting to lift and I was able to have a little fun, but something else took its place.

"Turn to page 243 in your text and I will discuss." I heard the professor, but my mind started to race. Even though I told myself to just sit still and take notes, I couldn't. I jumped up, grabbed my bags and ran as fast as I could to my dorm. Once inside I curled up in a ball and started to cry. I reached for the phone and called my mother. My mother was doing better; she had left Miami to start a new life in Alaska. She had finally gotten off crystal meth. Alcohol still held on, but meth was gone. For the first time since I was about six I felt like I had a little bit of a mom.

"Mom, thank God you're there." I was still in a ball and put the phone inside my legs so that I didn't have to hold it with my hands. "Jules, what's wrong?" I replied, "I don't know, Mom. I just had to run and now I can't stop crying and I feel like I can't do it Mom, I can't do it, but I have nowhere to go! I don't have a home and Grandma doesn't want me to move back there and I'm scared of Dad, but I don't think I can do this. All these kids have parents that dropped them off and decorated their dorms and mine looks like a prison, my side of the room is gray, I don't know how to decorate, do you decorate, Mom? I feel like I'm in prison, I don't want to be in prison and I don't have anyone and I just don't know what to do! No one likes me, I don't want to be weird anymore! Come and get me, please! I want to go home, but I don't have a home, Mom. It hurts so bad, my stomach hurts so bad, Mom, it hurts; it really hurts."

By this time my face had swollen from all the tears and snot was on my hands, face and the side of my leg. My mom started to talk to me in between my sobs, but I didn't really hear anything until she yelled, "Dammit Jules, you sound like my sister! Knock it off, you are having a panic attack. Take a deep breath and don't worry about doing or not doing anything. Just get a hold of your breathing." I had started to hyperventilate and my Mom knew it; she was trying to get me to take deep breaths. "Jules, breathe in and hold it. Now let it out. It's okay." I worked on breathing for about forty minutes, and then it was over.

The panic attacks started to happen to me about once a week. I didn't have any warning; I would just have to run to my dorm, call my Mom and cry and cry until I got my breathing back to normal, and then I would be so exhausted I'd say goodbye to my mother and lie in my bed for a two-hour nap. I went to the school doctor, but he didn't seem to think it was that big of a deal.

My emotional tank was getting low. It was as if my body way saying, "Hey; I can't take much more, don't you see this fucking blinking light? The light, the one that says 'Emotional Tank'." Have you ever seen someone walking on the side of the freeway with the gas can and you thought, "That's stupid, didn't they see the Low Fuel Light come on?" With all kidding aside, this is exactly what my brain was telling me: "Jules, you cannot take much more, you cannot take any more, you just can't handle it."

I didn't understand what was happening to me and I did not know how to take care of myself. As a child your parents teach you how to soothe yourself. They teach when to say yes to things and when it's a good idea to say no. Parents teach you boundaries and how to love and care for yourself. I learned how to dodge drunk fathers and save mothers from being raped and where to find my sister on my bicycle when she was drugged out and would call me. I learned that no one is going to help you; I learned that the world we live in is hell. I learned how to zone out and how to cry a lot. I didn't know how to parent myself; I was never parented. How can you learn what you were not taught?

The summer before my sophomore year I had decided to lose weight, and by the time school started I had lost my baby fat. It turns out that I didn't get my wish as a child in Mexico. I did inherit the Glass beauty curse, but not on the same beauty level as my mother and her mother before her. I was gifted with a lesser version, and whatever I lacked in beauty I made up with in my tiny waist, big breasts and full lips. These other attributes were all physical traits of my father's side of the family. The male sex began to notice me, and I liked the attention. I always wanted a lean athletic body, but curves have always been something I have never been able to get rid of. In fact, I started to just get attention from all angles. People started to overlook my awkwardness, and the only thing that I knew was different about me was that I was twenty-five pounds lighter. This was attention that I did not want to lose, so eating became something I did on an every other day occasion and usually only a handful of chicken or a 1/2 cup of cottage cheese.

I tried to do well in school, but my mind was not able to focus for long. I felt like an electric screwdriver that doesn't have a full charge. Have you ever started a big project that needed a power screwdriver and when you got it you realized it wasn't fully charged? So you plug it in for an hour and think it will be ready to use. At first after the hour of charging it's great and you think, cool, it's charged. Then about a minute or two later it starts to die. I was the uncharged screwdriver, no pun intended. I would sit in class and it wasn't like when I was a kid and I wanted to zone, I really wanted to listen, but my brain just didn't let me. I had a professor in Biology class who would catch me on my way out of his class and say, "Jules, are you okay?" I always thought it was weird, but I think he knew I was losing it.

I majored in audio engineering. Some of the best music industry agents, managers and audio engineers came out of this school. They had a music industry association that help navigate throughout the industry and gave students the opportunity to intern and learn about the jobs hands on. As soon as I found the flyer I signed up. Later that night I got a call from a woman named Heidi. "So Jules, I see you just signed up for our organization and I wanted to welcome you. We have a meeting tomorrow night and as the president of the organization I wanted to personally say welcome and invite you."

I couldn't wait for the meeting; I just knew I was going to be the best audio engineer ever. The meeting had about one hundred kids. This cute little redhead went to the front and introduced herself as Heidi Noore. What kind of name was that, I thought. As soon as she started talking I was mesmerized. I can still remember her maroon silk button-up shirt. She sat on top of a desk, kicking her legs and talking about the organization. As soon as she was done and the meeting was over I made a beeline to her and introduced myself. "Hello! I'm Jules Alexander, and I'm going to be an audio engineer." Heidi greeted me and said something to the effect of me having a lot of energy. "How can I help, Heidi? I want to help." She was kind of taken aback my me and said, "Well, this weekend we are meeting downtown to be extras on the "Jealous Bone" video with Patty Loveless. Would you like to come?" I think my feet actually might have elevated a bit as I jumped like a schoolgirl. "Yes! Yes, I can do that."

Heidi was 24 and was a junior in college. She had joined the Air Force just out of high school so that she could get her college paid for. She had been raised by a single mom named Shirley. Shirley was a teacher at a cosmetology school; she'd raised Heidi without any help from Heidi's father. Shirley had impeccable taste; everything she touched smelled good and looked good. Shirley passed this on to her child; Heidi could take a cardboard box and make it look like a mansion. Heidi was driven, passionate and knew what she wanted and how she was going to get there. She also had really big boobs, too; in the end it's all about the boobs, isn't it?

The weekend came and I showed up at the correct spot with the other 20 or so students. Heidi got all the access passes and we went in the club where they were going to shoot the video. I made a point to say hi to her and thank her for allowing me to come. Even though she was unsure of me she made a point to stand next to me and talk. We hit it off instantly, or so I thought; if you asked her she might say that it took a bit longer for her. "Hold on Jules, I'll be right back." Heidi left to talk to some woman with a clipboard, said a couple of things and came right back. She told me that the model who was supposed to go on the stage with a male model next to Patty hadn't shown up. They had seen me and wanted to use me in her place and asked if I was interested. Holy shit, I thought, of course I was interested! How fucking exciting was that! So for a night I was a model and got to dance with this beautiful man and watch how they made videos. It was a cool experience, and if you look really close in the video you can see my blonde ass dancing up a storm.

I wanted so much to be a part of Heidi's group. Heidi had three friends who always hung out together: Cale, the treasurer of the organization; Betty, the Secretary; and Erin, the Vice President. Man, these guys were cool! But all I wanted to do was to get around Heidi. I didn't yet understand why; all I knew was that I felt like I had a force pushing me toward her.

So, how do you get closer to Heidi? Why, you date her best friend Cale, of course. Cale and I went out a couple of times. He took me the CMA awards and some cool places, but it was like with most of the guys I dated: blah.

Thanksgiving break was coming and everyone was going home. I didn't want to be in the gray dorm alone. I was still having panic attacks, but not as much after I had started hanging out with Heidi. One day she said to me, "Jules, I'm not going home for Thanksgiving, you want to hang out?" Was that even a question! I think I would have walked through buckets of rattlesnakes if I got to spend time with this amazing woman.

Break came and the first day off Heidi called me: "You want to go to Nashville later and catch a movie?" We set a time for me to go over to her apartment about five. I took three showers and curled my hair until it was begging me to stop. When I could do no more to make myself beautiful I looked at the clock; it was only 1pm. I just couldn't wait anymore; I got in my car and drove to Heidi's. She opened the door and said, "Holy shit! I must have fallen asleep, I'm so sorry! I don't want us to be late, come on in." With that she ran to her bedroom, shut the door to get ready and then came out confused to inform me it was only 1:15pm. "Well, I don't like to be late, what can I say. I'm bored, Heidi, let's go now." She laughed.

As I look back on my life, the signs have always been there, but I never knew until that night that I was attracted to women. To tell you the truth, I could have been one who got married and had seven kids and didn't learn about my sexuality until my kids were grown. I had sex appeal that men liked, and I still do. It's funny; now that I'm open about my sexuality people expect that I'm a certain way and they even try and put me in their little boxes. I have a guy at work who always makes a comment about my painted toenails and open-toed shoes and says something each time a wear a skirt, "Oh look, Jules, you're in a skirt. Wow." The fact is that I wear skirts more than the other women in the office. The other fact is that if you remove my title as "lesbian" I'm more feminine than most women in my office. But it seems out of the ordinary, so people are shocked that I have feminine qualities and I'm a lesbian. When I was younger I used to be even more feminine, and because I got so much attention from men I never questioned my sexuality. I was left to assume that the right one had not come along, and without Heidi I might have met a man who I connected with or thought I connected with and married him. I could totally see that. I had sex with a couple of men before Heidi and it was okay;

not bad, nothing earth shaking. It was sex. It felt good, and if I had never met Heidi, I would have never known the difference. We sat on her couch for several hours before we headed to the movies. We talked about nothing, but it was great. I was so excited. "Where are we going? Oh, I heard about this theater! Oh my god, I'm so excited." Heidi laughed at my eagerness to watch a movie with her.

At the theater we got our tickets and sat down. The movie started. She had her legs up in the seat in from of her. I looked at her knee and I had to stop myself from putting my hand on the inside of her thigh. That though surprised me; I shook my head, thinking how weird it was. After the movie we headed home. Heidi stopped on our way and got us some wine. As we started to go up the stairs to her apartment I stopped halfway and said, "I'll be right back." I went to my car to get a piece of gum, thinking, "In case she kisses me I want to have fresh breath." I went from leaning over the driver's seat digging to find a gum to sitting in the driver position and staring over the steering wheel. "What?" I said aloud, "What?" I sat there silent for several minutes.

When I went back up to the apartment Heidi handed me my wine glass. She talked and talked and talked and talked, and I have no idea what she was saying. It was as if my sexuality was just given the key to a door I had not known existed until that night. I allowed myself to smell her perfume; I stared at her breasts, ivory skin and amazingly sexy neck. I knew she was saying words, but all I saw was her lips pressed against her wine glass and how they stuck a little each time she pulled away. I only had this revelation an hour earlier, but I couldn't contain it.

Once I had realized it I could not be contained an hour longer. In the middle of her sentence I took her wine glass from her hands and lowered it to the table. She looked at me with confusion. I moved toward her until I was able to straddle her. I removed my blouse and bra to expose my breasts without a word. I looked directly at her. "Do you want to touch me?" "Yes," she replied quickly and breathless. I grabbed her hands and put them on my breasts. I leaned over to her ear and said, "Then you can."

Thanksgiving week was amazing. We never left each other's side. Her roommate Cale, the one I was dating, had gone home for the holiday, so we had the apartment to ourselves. We talked for hours, made love for hours. I was turned on the entire week over everything she did. I finally knew what everyone had always talked about. This euphoric feeling of being in love; it was like we were on drugs. We took drives and I would unbuckle myself so that I could lie on her lap as the passenger side felt too far away. We would drive for hours, and I would fall asleep while she was driving. She would take me to places I never knew existed. I was in awe of this incredible woman.

I could only go so long without touching her, and if it went past a certain point I had to have her. It didn't matter if we were driving or in the grocery store I had to have her. At first she didn't think I was being serious, but after a couple of times convincing her I was serious on the freeway and at the movies she knew I wasn't kidding and made sure she got me to a place that would not get us both arrested. In the following months we fell deeply in love.

Thanksgiving week passed and Cale came back. Heidi didn't know how to handle it. We didn't want to sleep without each other. We had gone a lifetime sleeping alone, and after six days all we knew was that we couldn't survive without having our naked bodies sleeping side by side. Heidi would wait for Cale to go to sleep and then signal me to come in. We did this successfully for some time.

When school started back up I had a difficult time being away from her. She seemed to do fine and was super excited to see me at the end of the day, but I didn't have such a good time without her. I was still having a hard time concentrating in classes, and I found myself wandering the campus and avoiding my classes. I was great when we were together, but apart I was still dealing with this low emotional tank.

Christmas time came and she wanted to take me home to Illinois. She planned a little trip through a bigger city to stop by a gay bar. I looked at her strangely when she said that. "Gay" bar? What? "Jules, we are two woman having sex – that's gay." I knew she was right, but it just didn't sit right with me. I began to think that everyone knew what we were doing, and it clicked another level lower in my emotional tank.

Heidi was in a much better place to deal with her sexuality, I was her first woman, too, but she was 24 and I was eighteen. We stopped in the big city, checked into a motel and went to this "gay bar". When we walked up to the door and you would have thought Heidi was going home to all her "people". I, on the other hand, was not. We went through the front door and saw an older slender man wearing a lot of black leather. He looked at us and said, "Ten dollars." Heidi paid, grabbed my hand and yanked me to the bar.

She was so excited that she failed to notice all the men half dressed in leather. Whips were placed on walls as decoration and it smelled manly. I scanned the bar. I didn't see one woman all; I saw was men, and the men were all looking at us. "Hey, can we get a drink?" The bartender put our drinks in front of us and said, "You girls probably want to go down the street. This is a leather sex bar, and unless one of you has a penis you better drink these and get out of here." The whole gay/lesbian integration had not taken place yet. Lesbians had their place and fags had theirs. It wasn't until fags started dying from AIDS and the only people there to take care of them were lesbians when this did change. Now you go to a gay/lesbian club and it's all mixed evenly, sprinkled with some straight people as well.

I begged Heidi to go back to the motel, but she wanted to go to the lesbian club. Once we had found the bar Heidi got us some drinks and we sat in the corner. Heidi didn't allow us to be wallflowers for too long. She has an electric personality, and if she is around people they usually want to be by her. Her presence is something that I had never seen before, or since. People are drawn to her like a magnet. It wasn't long until lesbians surrounded our table. "These women are scary to me," I whispered in Heidi's ear. But she didn't listen and kept up conversations. "I know they are probably really nice people, but I'm not comfortable. Can we leave?" She shook her head and said, "Relax, Jules. These are woman just like us." What? I thought, I shave and wear makeup! These women are nothing like me. Soon after Heidi got up to go the bathroom. I asked her to please not go. When she left I felt like an oddity and out of place. One woman tried to start a conversation with me: "Well you're a little cutie, how old are you, sexy?" I didn't say anything. I just jumped up out of my seat and ran to the bathroom. "Please, can we go Heidi? Please take me back to the motel." She said yes and I buried my face in her neck trying to hide from embarrassment when we exited the bar.

I was the strangest combination of a person at this time. I was like a child in so many ways, but I was beyond my age in sexuality. With Heidi I wavered between a woman and a child. I was at two extremes: a sexual powerhouse and yet still a little girl. I confused Heidi for good reason. She took me back to the motel and tried to talk to me about what happened, but I closed up. "Sweetie, we are having a lesbian relationship. Those women were just like us." She was trying to explain something that I did not want explained.

I was fine with Heidi alone and without society looming in, but I was not ready to jump into the gay/lesbian community and declare my citizenship just yet. To this day I do not feel connected to the gay community, and back then I certainly wasn't.

The next day we continued to Heidi's hometown. We showed up at her mom's house early in the afternoon. As soon as I walked in I knew the person living in this house was related to Heidi. It was a modest home, but decorated with such detail and class. Heidi didn't look much like her mother, but she had all her mannerisms. Shirley was a nice hostess, and I enjoyed getting to know her. She made up two different rooms for us and Heidi announced that we would be sleeping together. Her mom thought it was odd, but I don't think she really understood. Heidi's mother was a born again Christian in the worst way. Heidi on the other hand was a "fuck you and your righteous beliefs"-kind of person. I was in the middle, whatever. Heidi always wanted to push the envelope for acceptance, and she pushed it with me there.

"Please Heidi, I'm begging you again, just let it go." Heidi wanted to come out to her mother, but I didn't want to have to deal with the emotional drain that came with coming out. Plus, I wasn't sure I was a "True" lesbian and I hadn't yet figured it all out for myself. Heidi might have realized she was a lesbian, but I just realized I was in love with Heidi, and that was enough stress for me. I knew that sex with Heidi was amazing and I knew I was in love with her, but what did that mean? I didn't automatically wake up after sex with Heidi and go, "Yep, I'm a lesbian, pass the gay flag! I need to place it above every aspect of life." I was in love with Heidi. That's all I knew.

She did it. Of course; what did I expect? It was Heidi after all. She came out to her mother, and there was screaming and yelling. Her mother actually pointed at me and said something to the fact of me doing this "lesbian" thing to her daughter. Oh my god, I thought, fuck, what if I did? I did seduce her. Great, lady, thanks! That's all I needed. After a bit of yelling Heidi grabbed my arm and pulled me out the door and into her car. Looking back, she grabbed my arm and yanked me away many times. I just followed the Heidi bus wherever it took me. To those who know me now it would be funny to hear how dominant this woman was over me. Not too many people are more dominant than me, but Heidi was, and I just followed.

The next month Heidi negotiated a benefit that for us. Each year this association puts together a function for the music industry executives. They throw a shindig and it's an extravaganza; shows, dinners, awards. Heidi negotiated to have five people from our school go. If we did a good job as interns this would be an annual thing and the next year it would involve us as the major supplier of interns. This was a big deal and everyone at our school wanted to go. Heidi chose me, Cale, Erin and Betty.

As we got to New Orleans for the week of events I started to have panic attacks again. They had gone away, but had recently started back up, and I was trying to do my best with them. All of us met the CEO at this association at a New Orleans restaurant. This guy was disgusting. He was a fat, ugly, chauvinist pig. When we showed up at the restaurant to meet him I wasn't feeling well, but when did I feel well at that time? The only time I was having fun was when I was either having sex with Heidi or lying naked next to Heidi and talking. "Who is this cute blonde you have here," he asked. "A little young! Is she over eighteen?" I looked at him like he was bowl of vomit. Oh God, this guy was awful. "Yes, she is over eighteen," Heidi said. "Well, then she can sit by me." Heidi pushed me to sit

Jules Alexander

next to him. Needless to say I was pissed after we left.
On our way back to the hotel I let her have it. All of Heidi's friends
were scratching their heads as to why I was so pissed at her. They
didn't understand that to me it felt like that she was serving her
lover up as a pawn on a chessboard. It didn't feel right. I didn't wait
until we were alone. "What was that? Hey, let's take it a step
further! Why don't you take me to one of your "lesbian" bars and
you can pawn me off to some bull dyke so you can get a discount
on drinks?" I was right with being upset, but it wasn't the right time.
She grabbed my arm firmly and pulled me to our hotel room.
Needless to say after that everyone in our little clique knew we
were better than really "good" friends.
When we had our intern meeting the next day this man showed up
again. He announced that he felt more comfortable with Cale in
charge of the interns and not Heidi. He made some excuse, but it
clearly was because she was a woman. I stood up in front of about
25 people and let him have it. Keep in mind this man was very
influential within the music industry. I don't remember exactly what I
said, but it had something to do with "small penis size," being able
to find his penis over his fat belly, "male chauvinist" was thrown in a
couple of times, and asking him exactly how much extra does he
have to have to pay to get a whore to sleep with him. Heidi just
buried her head, shaking it from one side to the next.
I left and went back to the hotel. Heidi stayed and tried to smooth
everything over. They came up with a plan to let Cale run
everything. I wasn't allowed back. Heidi is an amazing negotiator;
it's no great surprise she went on to be a successful agent and then
manager in the music industry.
  I spent the remainder of the five days in the hotel room. After the
event we all had planned to go to Alabama, where Allison's family
had a house on the beach. No one was talking to me. This was a
big deal for all of the other students back at university; this event
housed a lot of executives that could make or break careers. They
were all doubtful that we would be asked back the next year due to
my outburst.
When we got to Alabama Heidi told me that everyone wanted to
talk to me. I sat at a campfire while four people told me how I
ruined their lives. As I look back on it now it was quite dramatic,
and if I had had the maturity I have now I would have stood up and
said, "Listen guys, I'm sorry I messed up, but five minutes a piece
is sufficient. A two-hour session on how I caused lives to be ruined
is an overkill." But I didn't have the maturity, so I took it and Heidi
let me take it. My emotional tank clicked a couple of levels lower.

In Alabama Heidi and I decided to keep our relationship a secret.
But when we returned to school Heidi decided, without telling me,

that she was going to come out to the entire school. Heidi was not a wallflower and she was extremely prominent within this school. If you put two and two together, it would come back to me as her lover. Wherever Heidi was I was, and vice versa. She outed me to the entire school. I know she was trying to understand her own feelings and take ownership of who she was, but I was in no shape to stand with the gay flag above my head. My emotional tank clicked one more level lower.

In the following four weeks I had several traumatic things happen to me at once. They went in this order:

"Jules! Hey, it's Laurie. I got your report card. You fell below at 2.0. If you get another report card below a 2.0 you will lose your trust fund money for school." I knew that my grades were not going to be above 2.0, and that meant I wasn't going to be able to take summer classes. If I wasn't able to take summer classes I didn't have a place to live. I knew I would have to go back to my dad's. My emotional tank clicked one more level lower.

"Jules, it's your mother. I know what's going on with this Heidi girl, and it's wrong and disgusting. You should be ashamed of yourself; you are too pretty to be gay. This woman is brainwashing you. Don't bother calling me anymore if you are gay. By the way, I told your granddad about this, and he told me to tell you that you are no longer his granddaughter if you choose this lifestyle." My emotional tank clicked one more level lower.

"Grandma, it's Jules. Can I talk to Granddad?" Click. I called back. "Grandma, can I please talk to Granddad?" "Jules, if you are a lesbian, and from what your mother is saying you are, you are no longer a member of this family. Granddad will not talk to you." Called back three hours later. "Hello?" "Granddad, it's me. Jules." "I don't know a Jules." Click.

"Jules, it's your dad. Your sister just told me that you are using my grandfather's money to pay for college; you've been lying to me about this the whole time. I told you if you ever used any of that money I would disown you. Don't you ever call me again, you piece of shit." Summer was a couple weeks away and I now had lost another option regarding where to live for the summer. My emotional tank clicked one more level lower.

"Do you see her over there, ya she's Heidi Noore's lover, what a waste, she's so pretty, fucking dyke, she's going to rot in hell." My emotional tank clicked one more level lower.

I started to have major panic attacks again and I would go to Heidi's classes and pull her out. When we were driving I would jump out of her car and just start to run. I don't know why; I just wanted my brain to stop. My childhood had not given me any foundation to handle these kinds of situations. Just a couple of these things happening to someone from loving stable parents would have had a hard time with. I didn't know what to do with these feelings, and I didn't know how to handle them.

One afternoon I convinced the janitor of the building to let me into Heidi's office. I didn't want to get her out of class again, but I didn't want to be alone in my dorm. I didn't turn on the light. I don't know why; I just pulled the seat out from under the desk and curled up under it. Heidi opened her office to find me under her desk curled up in a ball in the pitch black sobbing and shaking uncontrollably. I know she regrets it and she didn't understand what was going on, but she told me that day, "I don't want to do this anymore Jules. You are too emotional." All my options were gone. I was going to be homeless in a matter of two weeks. I didn't have a dad, mom, or trust fund. My college days were over, I was laughed at on campus, I didn't have a granddad, and now I had lost Heidi.

I left her office, and at that moment my emotional tank finally clicked to empty. I got into my car and drove to ten different pharmacies. I got three bottles of Tylenol Night Time liquid at each pharmacy – 30 bottles in total. I went back to my dorm room. I opened up all the bottles, poured all the pills on the bed and started taking as many as I could get into my mouth. After about 20 minutes I started vomiting. When I finished vomiting I started taking more pills; I vomited again. I did this over and over again until I got all of them down. This was not an attempt; if I had had a gun I would be dead right now and not writing this book. I was not joking. I wanted out of this miserable life. I had nothing left.

Heidi decided that she was too harsh on me and thank God she did, because I was unconscious when she found me. I remember short snippets of that night. I remember a big doctor pulling me up by my shirt and smacking me, saying, "You don't have the right to do this, this is God's choice! Wake up little girl." Another memory is when this doctor sits me up and tells the nurse, "Make her drink it, do it!" The doctor was mad at me and I don't know why, but it shocked me and made me try to stay awake. I remember the black gritty drink that tasted like tires and how it ran out of my mouth and onto my breast. I remember the doctor talking to Heidi and asking her if I had any family here. "No, she doesn't really have family." I wanted to scream, "My sister! I have my sister still, I have her!" But I couldn't get it out.

I don't know when exactly, but when I woke my eyes were heavy. I looked directly above me and saw a camera. I looked toward the door and saw another camera. I felt a familiar body lying next to me on the bed. Heidi stayed with me the entire time I was in the hospital; she never left my side. "Hey, how are you?" I tried to focus my eyes and asked, "Where am I?" When she told me that I was in the hospital all I could think about was becoming my mother. "When can I leave?" Heidi informed me that I needed to speak with

the hospital psychiatrist and he would decide.
"So Jules, do you think you are depressed?" What is the hell kind of question is that to ask someone who has just tried to commit suicide? That's like asking an alcoholic if he would like a drink! I haven't spent one day in a psych class, but I can most definitely say depression has something to do with all suicide attempts. So my reply clearly was, "No, I'm not depressed." He asked, "Are you going to try this again?" "Nope." What a dingle berry, a total piece of shit that has encrusted on a ball sack, that is what that man was.

Heidi took me back to her apartment. I didn't tell anyone in my family. Why in heaven's name should I? the only one still talking to me was my sister. When I came out to my sister she said verbatim, "Dude, do you think I'm a lesbian too? No, I like dick too much. But it's cool." That was the extent of our conversation. Nothing more was said after that. We gathered that I was a lesbian and that Jennifer liked dick too much to be a lesbian. Enough said.

Heidi found me a lesbian therapist who worked on a sliding scale. I think she charged me five dollars a session. She focused on my coming out as my issue, but it was much deeper. I had a huge fear of intimacy, and even though I loved Heidi with all my heart she was a major cause of my anxiety at the time. At first she helped with the excitement and euphoric feeling, but as time went on she scared the shit out of me with "forever's," and my fear of being close started my anxiety up again. Heidi did not have a soothing soul. She tried, but she was not able to calm me down. If I didn't react the way she wanted she would get angry, and anger to me is like poison. To this day, if someone gets angry at me or raises their voice I turn into a little girl inside. What I've learned is to tell whoever it is to lower their voice or I will leave. But if you looked inside you would see a little blonde girl with green eyes crying.

I don't know how to explain the raw emotion of depression. It's an awful feeling and no matter what you do, nothing helps it. About three weeks later I was talking about killing myself again. Heidi took me to the hospital where they checked me in. I spent seven days there. They did every test you can imagine and they came up with "coming out issues". I wish I could go back; as an adult I would walk through the hospital and ask for credentials, because there is no way these fucking idiots had any schooling of any kind. They discharged me; Heidi was devastated because she was scared.

Jennifer called me a day or so later and I told her everything. "Jules, you need to come stay with me for a while." Jennifer was working on a cow farm in the middle of nowhere in Washington. She was trying to get sober, and she thought the middle of nowhere was a good idea. She was right; she got off drugs in this time in her life. After we had spoken my mother called me and spouted her love for me; she wanted me to come stay with her in Alaska. I told her I wanted to go to Jennifer's instead. My mother had not been there for me since I had been six. Sure, she was off meth, but she still called me drunk off her rocker about once every two weeks. I didn't want to have to deal with her shit and mine as well. My mother bought me a ticket to Washington.

When I arrived my sister was taken aback by my weight. My eyes were sunken and I looked sick. She took me back to the farm and tried desperately to help me, but I had hit a place beyond talking. I sat on her couch and just cried. One day I started plucking all my eyelashes and eyebrows out. My hair started falling out and Jennifer realized that I was way beyond what she could do. She called my father and explained to him that his "disowning" thing would have to be put on hold because I needed him. After five minutes of explaining to my dad what was going on he booked me the next flight to Miami.

Chapter 9
Recovering with Dad

I walked into the airport lobby when I saw my dad. As soon as his eyes met mine he put his hand over his mouth like my sister had done years earlier. He too was trying to make sure crazy wasn't going to get into his mouth. My skin was pale, a pale you would see with a cancer patient. My eyes looked strange without any eyebrows or eyelashes. I looked like I was dying. My weight had dropped to the point that my bones were protruding through my clothes. My dad started to cry, but stopped himself because he saw my tears first and didn't want to be the cause of any more. "Can you walk, Jules? Do you need me to carry you?" I didn't say anything; I just shook my head to tell him no.

He started to make small talk as we went to get my bags. I noticed everyone looking at me. At one point my father noticed and blurted to a man, "What are you looking at?" I started to cry. I couldn't handle any anger and my dad apologized. "I won't do that again, Jules." He put his arm around me and pulled me toward him. I gave him most of my weight and we walked to his truck.

My father continued to make small talk as we drove home. I didn't respond. I just looked out the window with my head bobbing to the motion of the truck. "You want a hamburger, Jules? In-N-Out Burger is just over there. I'm going to get you one." I didn't respond, and once he got the burgers he put them on my lap. I didn't move and as soon as he turned out of the parking lot they fell off. I didn't make any attempt to catch them. The rest of the ride home my dad didn't say anything else, and neither did I. I looked out the window and let the tears roll off my face.

The next month or so my dad took me to and from tons of doctor's appointments. He settled on sending me to a tiny female redheaded psychiatrist. She did dozens of tests on me and never came up with any imbalances of any kind. My dad drove me every other day, filled my prescriptions and gave them to me like a child.

"Barbara, what do you think is wrong with me?" She didn't play the usual therapist shit by saying, "What do you think is wrong with you?" She knew I was not at that level, so she tried to break it down to me: "Jules honey, you just had enough and your mind gave out. The human brain can only take so much stress before it gives. It's not mental illness that you are afraid of, it's just your body saying ENOUGH. The good news is, everything you shared with me tells me that you will come out of this. Soon we will find the right antidepressant, and it will kick in and some of the pressure will lift. When it does we can try to purge the rest in therapy. But for now all

I want you to do is breathe and eat. These are the only two things I want you to focus on, okay?"

I started waking up screaming. It took my dad two seconds to be by my bed to hold me, saying, "It's okay little one, Daddy's here." I believe my dad would wait for me to go to bed and then he would fall asleep by my bed. Over time these went from a nightly occurrence to once or twice a week. But whenever they happened he was there.

During the day he would get me up and take me to the beach. I have always liked the beach. Sometimes I walked into the ocean and sometimes he put me over his shoulder and walked for me. He waited with me for a wave and then put me on the board to ride it. If it was a good one I would smile a little and he would say, "Aw, I saw a smile, Jules. Let's catch another." He would do this for hours with me. The antidepressants started to kick in and we started to have a little fun. "Hey Julia, let's go skeet shooting." I tilted my head a bit. "Dad, are you crazy, dude? I'm suicidal, remember?" He shook his head like he had forgotten and we laughed. We went shooting that day and I hit every skeet, the only time I ever did that. My dad was pumped, thinking I was going to be a professional.

My dad was the only one who didn't know I was gay. When I finally told him he was the only one who reacted how you would want someone who loves you to react. He then told me stories of his father. "When I was a twelve I looked like I was sixteen, and my mother would make me drive and get my dad in gay bars. He was so ashamed of it, and I believed he married my mother to cover it up. Things were different back then, Jules. You are tiny like my father; maybe you got this from him as well. Jules, if this is what this is all about then don't be like my dad. Be proud of who you are." I was trying to process this is my mind without the pressure of Heidi, and it was hard to figure out. I still had some attraction for men and I would declare different labels. My dad was consistent with love and his reaction to my coming out. Every so often I would declare a different label: "Dad, I think I'm bisexual." To which my father would say, "Cool, means you have 50% better chance of getting a date on Saturday." A day or so would go by. "Dad, I think I'm a lesbian." He would reply, "Well, I understand. Women are mesmerizing. I don't know why all women aren't gay." He just let me talk to him, and it was the first time I talked to him and processed life.

My dad spent every minute of the day with me for several weeks. He never gave up; he never wavered; he never missed a cry; he never missed a time when I needed him. At first I didn't have the strength to care if he was going to freak out and start his bullshit. But as time went on and the antidepressants started helping, I got concerned. I knew that it was only a matter of time, and I was not even close to being able to handle it. I spent a couple of days at this time trying to hide the fact that things were lifting. Crazy, but I didn't want to lose the Good Dad. As time went on I couldn't help it, and my dad could tell I was feeling better. He was so happy.

Even though it was nice to have all the attention I wanted to get back to feeling like an adult. "Jules, why don't you take the truck to go to your doctor's appointment this afternoon?" "Can I, Dad?" My dad had two trucks at the time, a silver 1979 Ford F150 and a brand new truck with absolutely everything you could have on it. He had talked about getting this truck for years. "When I get my inheritance I'm going to get a Blue F150 with pin stripes and loaded with everything. It's going to have this engine—" blah blah blah. Jennifer and I had heard about this truck he was "going" to have for about ten years. So I was surprised when he said, "Ya, you can take the blue truck."

I started to take the blue truck by myself every time I needed to go to the doctors. So when Barbara suggested that I go to some "Children of Alcoholics" classes I asked my dad if I could take the truck. He asked where I would be going. I told him the truth and he said, "You bet, little one." My dad realized the damage he had done and was not affected by me trying to help myself navigate through what his and my mother's drinking and drug abuse had done. When I left that day to go to the class he said, "I'm proud of you, little one." I didn't want to go, though, because I felt like I was cheating on my father. But I went.

Every time I sat with Barbra I would regurgitate my childhood, thinking it would heal me somehow. She would suggest things like, "I would like you to journal." I would do it; whatever she asked, I would do it. But getting better was the hardest thing I have ever done in my life. Most days, charging a brain that has become uncharged felt like fighting a losing battle. Even though I was out of the staring-into-space phase and the continued crying, I still had such a huge fog. The antidepressants were helping, but I never had the "the clouds lifted and I felt like my old self"-verbiage that you see on all the antidepressant commercials. Of course now I realize that being bipolar II is quite a bit different than clinical depression. I think Barbara had an idea and suggested that I try Lithium, but I drew a line in the sand: "I am not bipolar, I am not like my mother. If you say that to me again, I will not come back." Barbara probably knew that it would not have been a good idea for me not to return, so she dropped it. I was a little better, and that was leaps and bounds from everyone wondering if I needed to be hospitalized for an indefinite time. My father said, "I will be her hospital. Tell me what you need me to do and I'll do it. She is my job, I am her father."

Barbara said something to me that stuck in my head, "Jules, fake it until you make it." I put that phrase in my brain and I started to highlight it in my head when I wanted to jump off a bridge. It's not that I didn't want to; I knew that I would probably not be successful. Killing yourself is harder than most think. Not being successful meant that I would go back to the hospital, or that my dad would not let me drive alone or do anything I wanted to. I also started to learn that if you hold tight to those bad thoughts and you don't act on them they eventually go away. If you react to the bad thoughts, it just makes things worse. When they go away, you get to feel better for a little bit until the bad thoughts come back. In the beginning this was hard because the bad thoughts overpowered the good thoughts. But as time went on, the bad would go down and the good would stay a bit longer. I never felt leveled; I just knew that if you hold on long enough, you will get to the good feeling.

With my newfound freedom I started to explore the gay bars in Miami. There was one that I loved: it was a country-dancing bar, and I would sneak in and dance from 8pm until they closed. I would have a blast when I was there. I would find a woman who was attractive, and then I locked on to the target and figured out how to get her in bed. This would keep an obsession in my mind and it would hold off the bad feelings for a bit longer.

One night I had one too many drinks and I crashed the side of my dad's precious truck. "Oh damn!" I thought, "Dad is going to flip." I thought about turning hard right on the freeway at 80 miles per hour on my way home. That way, if I lived he would be so happy I lived that he wouldn't flip out if I crashed the truck. I decided on going home and parking the truck and try to figure something out in the morning.

I didn't get the chance. "Jules!! Juliaaaaaaaaa!! Come here, Jules!" I tried to prepare myself. "Yes, Dad?" I could tell that he was trying so hard not to flip out. As I look back it's funny, but it wasn't at the time; I was thinking that he was going to lose it and I was going to be homeless again. The veins on his neck were popping and I was all too familiar with this look. I knew what was next and I prepared myself. I followed him around the truck to the side that was damaged. "Do you see this, Jules?" He started to incase just the damaged part with his hands, like Vanna White does with the letters. "This right here, do you see this?" He was trying so hard not to flip out it was comical. I started to laugh, just as my sister would have done. He started to laugh, too. "Well, I just wanted to make sure that you saw this part of the truck. Apparently some asshole drove up our driveway and hit this truck and fled into the night. Those bastards!" We busted out laughing and I agreed that they were assholes for not leaving a note. "Jules, it's just a truck. I can get it fixed. Are you okay?" "Yes Dad, thanks."

I've learned to be thankful for all things in my life. I am thankful for this breakdown, even though it was the hardest time in my entire life. I got to bond with my dad. I was such a sensitive child that his rage and abuse made me recoil into a recluse in my younger years. But my dad was always able to control his anger in emergency situations, and this was a prolonged emergency situation. My father talked with me about his childhood, and the more he talked the more I understood him. He would tell me stories of his mother beating him and he would make a joke out of it, but if you looked close you could see that little boy in his eyes, and it was sad. He told me about his struggle with dyslexia and how his parent's didn't help him learn to read. The only way he got through high school was because he was such a good athlete they would pass him so he could play baseball. He told me about how his mother kept beating him until he was sixteen and finally he told her he had enough, and he warned her many times to leave him alone. She never did, and my father broke his mother's nose on that night. That was when he stopped receiving beatings. His stories are not mine to tell, but I began to understand my father after this time.

These months I stayed with him he didn't drink as much, and he would stay up with me and watch TV. I would cuddle up to him and he would put his arm around me and tell me he loved me. We put in a sprinkler system together and a fence. We talked about his life as a child and many times when I went to bed I would ask "God" to hug my dad as a father and mother because he needed it. My father was a sad man and I never knew it; I just saw the raging. I wish I had seen it sooner.

After the summer I told my dad that I wanted to go back to college at a university. I called Laurie with his blessing and got a waiver from my great-grandma for my low GPA the last semester. My dad didn't think it was a good idea to go back, and Barbara didn't think it was a good idea either. But I didn't listen to either of them; I wanted to get back to Heidi and my adulthood again.

As soon as I drove to the campus I started to shake. I found my dorm, where I met Heidi and we started to unpack my things. The school, the smells, Heidi; everything was too much for me. My father and Barbara were right. I didn't want them to be right, but I called my dad. "Dad, I don't think I'm ready. Can I come home?" My dad just listened to me and said, "Are you sure? Or do you want me to come out for a couple of weeks in a hotel, so you know I'm close. Maybe that will help you get settled." My father flew out that day and we were eating at a restaurant together by the evening. Heidi came with me to the restaurant, and my father was open arms to her and us. After dinner my Dad told us he was going to his hotel, and to call him if I needed him. Six hours later I called. "Dad, I want to go back; I'm not ready." He never sighed and said, "Geez Jules, everyone bent over backwards to get you here, why don't you buck it up?" We left the next morning for Miami.

Over the next several months I got stronger and stronger. I learned two things during this process: "Fake it until you make it," and that my father loved me more than his rage. These lessons were worth the price and, as I stated above, I am thankful for this time in my life. That might be strange to hear with what I went through, but I've been as far as you can go down emotionally, and I came back up. Not many people can say that.

As I look back on this time I do think that being bipolar II did play a significant role in this breakdown, but I still think it would have happened to just about anyone. Emotional tanks are nothing to mess with. I check mine often now and make sure that I'm always putting in more than I'm taking out.

I did eventually move back to Nashville to be with Heidi, but the trauma of everything we had gone through proved too much for us and we broke up. I never went back to college. To this day, if I'm in a meeting room for more than an hour or so I will get a little panic attack and excuse myself. I know I could probably work through it, but it has never been a sincere desire for me to finish college.

Chapter 10
Sex Addiction

When I was outlining this book, I quickly wrote down the chapters. Chapter 1, "The Beginning"; Chapter 2, "Diagnosed Bipolar II With Rapid Cycling" and so on and so forth until I came to Chapter 9, "Sex Addition." I paused for several minutes and thought, "sex addiction" – where did that come from? My soul knew that it was true, and what I have always thought bubbled to the surface. I knew that an unmediated bipolar usually comes with an addiction of some sort. I had always figured I was a higher breed and smart enough to have slipped by this little nuance that follows most bipolar people, regardless of the type. It would be easier for me to write the names of the people in my family who were not addicted to alcohol or drugs than to name ones who were drug addicts or alcoholics. I told myself, "You don't do drugs, and you don't drink," so much in my life that I drifted down a different path altogether, convincing myself that I did not have the addiction infliction. I was wrong.

This is the one chapter that is going to be the most difficult for me. I tried to tell Melissa years ago, but she would never really hear what I was trying to say, and my fear and embarrassment would always stop me short. One night, when Melissa and I had been out together only a couple of times, I got up the nerve to tell her that I was propositioned by mostly straight woman all the time, and she laughed as we drove to a restaurant. She laughed so hard I dropped it and started laughing with her. But I was only telling the half-truth. As we walked through the dining room I caught the eye of a straight couple sitting at the bar, and once I saw the woman's eyes I knew what she was thinking. When I realized this, I looked away. Fifteen minutes later the woman comes up to the table and says that she and her husband would like to take me home, and if I was interested, here was their number. As the woman walked away Melissa started to laugh. "Julia, what the hell was that?" I shook my head and said that I had no idea. The truth was that I was all too familiar with this and so many other sex-capades that from this moment on I decided not to tell Melissa the whole truth about my life. This part of my life was too disgusting to someone as beautiful and glowing with positive rays of light as she was.

Let me also start this chapter with my true belief of sexuality. I identify as a lesbian only because that's what makes people feel comfortable. Society likes to take people by the nape of the necks and drop them into boxes that make them feel better. But the truth as I see it is that there are no "true" gay/lesbian people, just like there are no "true" straight people. But: "true" bisexuality is also a non-truth. Most people don't have the same attraction for women as they do for men, which would define "true" bisexuality. The truth is as I see it is that there are mostly straight people and mostly gay/lesbian people. But given the right setting and the right time and the right soul, we all can fall in love with the latter of our dominant attraction. For most people that's just too much to take, so they identify as gay or straight. What most people don't know about me is that I am open for love in whichever sex form it comes, but the odds are that it will be with a woman. But if love ever does come to me in the form of a man I would be a willing participant with the soul that draws me.

So as you read on, understand that I apologize about spouting my "lesbian" self, but it's what I've identified with to help eliminate making people feel uncomfortable. My apologies to the right-wing Christians for outing your perfect straight people theory. But I've slept with enough right-wing Christian, mostly straight women, and I feel like I'm speaking with a bit more experience than the hellfire-and-damnation preacher on Sunday. My apologies to the gay/lesbian/bisexual society for outing the fact that those three identifiers are incorrect as well. Humans come mostly straight and mostly gay, but as I've said above, "mostly" is not a definite. I also believe that this is why most gay/lesbian identifying people have a hard time coming out. To come out you have to deny all attraction for the opposite sex to be inducted into the gay culture. If you identify as bisexual you get the evil eye, like you are gross. What is gross in my opinion is to deny one's true self on any level, and I'm just as gross as the next gay, lesbian or straight bisexual out there. My true identity is mostly lesbian. My additional apologies for getting so deep, and for most it might be a bit too deep to accept, but if you really think and analyze this and hold yourself to no judgment of any kind, you will realize that I am right. I watched a movie recently that had the same concept of my feeling on sexuality. The movie is called "Elena Undone." When I started watching this it was as if I had written the book. It's an excellent movie and moves through the lives of people who have found their "soul mates," regardless of their gender. It's a very interesting movie about falling in love.

While I was in Miami recovering from my nervous breakdown I would sneak into lesbian bars and I slept with a handful of lesbians. I never wanted anything more than sex because I still had such feelings for Heidi. Once we had broken up I decided that I wanted to take a second chance on love. I was dating a college student who was heavily entrenched within the gay community. She was okay, but I wasn't really into her. I would sneak into the clubs in Nashville and was always disappointed with the selection. So I put an ad in the gay/lesbian paper. "Seeking attractive (keyword attractive) white lesbian to date." The day it was published I got a call from a woman named Lynette. She seemed nice on the phone, but I wasn't really into meeting with her that day because I was meeting with the other woman I was sleeping with. So we planned for the following weekend. We set a time and a place at a local gay restaurant in Nashville.

The day for the date came. I was walking quickly into the restaurant because I was about 30 minutes late when this dark-haired beauty stopped me in my tracks. I immediately sat down at this woman's table uninvited. If I was to list all the physical qualities that attract me to a woman, this woman had them. She was in her early 30s and had rich brown hair and eyes, with a lean body and a sun kissed tan. "I hope you are Lynette," I said, and she replied, "I hope you are Jules." This was instant attraction. Lynette was recently divorced and living with a woman when I met her. The living-with-a-woman part was not something that I was told, and to tell you the truth, at that moment I didn't care. This attraction was instant and strong and felt by both of us. We quickly found ourselves in her car with her body on top of mine and this first kiss lasted about two hours.

The next day Lynette called and we planned to go to a play with her friends. She picked me up and we went to the play and then to dinner with her friends. I was twenty at the time, and Lynette was thirty-something. Her friends were what you would call "high class" lesbians. One of her friends was the cousin of Al Gore and that made the meeting feel all that more impressive. We ended the date as we did the night before, with her body on top of mine in her car. She was sure of her sexual self and this was new to me; I enjoyed not being in control.

Lynette was a nurse and exactly what you don't picture when you think of a lesbian. She was feminine, bubbly and extremely seductive. I would have compared her to Sophia Loren. I was just a pup and unable to fight this sexual being on any level.

"Jules, I want to take you to my place." I knew that we couldn't go to mine because my father was visiting me and staying at my apartment, so I told her that I was okay with it. When she stopped the car she told me of her girlfriend. Man, what a mood killer that was. "Lynette, that's not cool. You should not be here." With that I got out of the car and found a way home.

Two weeks passed and I got a call from Lynette. "Jules, can we go out tonight? I've been thinking about you." Listen closely when I tell you this. I have had sex with and had attractions to many, many, many women in my life, but nothing was as strong as Lynette's sexual draw. I took a deep breath and I said everything that I didn't want to say. "Lynette, listen: you have a girlfriend, you should not be calling me and I respect myself and your girlfriend enough for you and me together." With that I hung up the phone and threw my hands up in the air and said, "Self, what in the hell did you do that for, you stupid woman!"

But I was proud of what I had done and decided to treat my high and mighty self to a local drag show at the fabulous gay bar downtown. This bar was four bars in one; it was a drag bar, a cowboy bar, dance bar and a piano bar all under the same roof. I snuck by the bouncer checking for IDs and I was in. I scanned the room to see where I wanted to go when my eyes met Lynette's across the bar. I quickly walked into the drag bar, hoping Lynette hadn't really seen me. I ordered a drink and sat down to enjoy the show. As soon as I took a sip a woman's lips landed on my neck. "Have you ever seen the south side of Nashville?" I replied "no" as the woman continued to kiss my neck. She said, "Would you like to?" I knew the voice. Lynette was not the type of woman that could be told no. I tried to resist, but as my neck tilted back I whispered, "yes." She grabbed my hands and placed them on her as I followed her to the parking lot and to her house. I was like a puppy in the hands of a sexual master. I don't know what we did that night; all I knew was that she had Mormon boys on their mission living below her, and they looked at me very strangely when our eyes met in the parking lot.

When I met Lynette I wandered through sex, and sometimes I did it right and sometimes it was probably comical. Lynette taught me how to really please a woman. She took her time, and everything was sensual and open and erotic. Nothing was off limits with this woman; nothing. I told her how I thought watching a woman dance was a turn-on for me. She listened, but didn't say anything. The next night I came to see her. I walked into her apartment lit with candles and erotic music playing. She came around the corner in a beautiful red negligee. Her Italian skin lit up the red to an even more intense color, and if that had been all that happened that night I would have been in heaven. She grabbed my hand without saying a word and undressed me. She put a funny device through my legs and finished it by locking a dildo on. I was pushed to a chair and my legs and arms were tied behind me so tightly that my fingers and ankles started to tingle within minutes. I could not move the slightest bit. Then she started to dance with the music and pleasured herself with the dildo that I had between my legs. This was the only time I have ever climaxed without a touch.

This woman was sexual pleasure in the finest form. Have you ever passed out by pure arousal? I have and it was in this woman's bed. I was just a kitten in a lioness's bed. I was no match for this sexual black belt and I fell fast. She broke it off with her girlfriend and we started an exclusive relationship – or that's what I was told. What was actuality was that she was sleeping with two other women besides me: one 43-old engineer and a 34- year old dental assistant. So when I found out about this I did what anybody would do: I stayed the night with her – come on, she was a sexual goddess and I didn't want to waste the last time I would sleep with her. But the next morning I told her what a horrible person she was and I left telling her I would not be coming over anymore. As I drove home I decided to make it my goal to find out who these two women were and set my sights on seducing both of them with my newfound abilities.

I would succeed. This was the beginning of my addiction. Lynette was to me like the first shot of heroin is to a future addict. I began chasing the "Lynette high" for years to come.

My first target was the 43-year old engineer. As with most of Lynette's prey, Debbie was attractive, feminine and bright. But, how was a 21-year old going to seduce a much older, classy, beautiful engineer? Lynette had a way of finding lesbians that were out of the ordinary. I realized early in life that going to the lesbian bars led you to a class of woman that neither intrigued nor enticed me. My idea of a woman is not a woman who wants to look like a man, but rather a woman who enjoys and embraces all the wilds of her femininity.

It wasn't hard to seduce Debbie and we connected on a real level. We spent nights watching movies and making love. Her home was soft and inviting, and I enjoyed the warmth that her soul created. "Jules, you are 21 and I am 43," she told me one day. "Regardless of our connection I am a short phase in your love life." I didn't understand her insight and I angered each time she brought this up. I believe she was trying to help me understand that our connection was true, but that it had an ending in sight. She was a kind soul and her insight was correct, but at the time I did not see if that way. All I knew was that I loved her.

As I look back this was perfect for me at the time; I had a real fear of intimacy. But although my fear was strong, I still had a childlike belief in love. What I didn't understand was my emotional cycle, and this would be a huge problem in my life. Debbie was there and enjoyed our time together. But, she also knew with maturity that what we had was not to be a lifelong relationship. Because she knew this she never let herself truly fall for me. I never felt threatened or trapped, and if I don't feel threatened or trapped I don't run.

This allowed me to continue our love affair for some time until a warm night in August. Debbie and I were out eating at local restaurant and she was spouting about what she always had and I finally told her that I wanted more. This was the first time that I said this instead of saying, "Whatever, Debbie." That night she ended our affair as gently as she could. She had begun dating a woman more close to her age, and with me demanding more she drew a line in the sand. I was not on the side with Debbie any longer. It was time and I can see that now, but as a 21- year old I didn't understand and got hurt.

I was getting tired of getting hurt in my life. Heidi had broken my heart, Lynette had broken my heart, Debbie had broken my heart, my mom had broken my heart, my dad had broken my heart, my granddad had broken my heart, life was breaking my heart. So, finally my heart broke. My emotional wall lifted each time my heart was broken and after Debbie only a couple more levels were left before the wall would lift and surround my entire body. I was starting to feel as if the only reason women wanted me around was to have sex with me. With the type of childhood I had and the addictive personality I had I embraced what I thought was my calling: to give everyone who wanted to sleep with me a chance to ride. It's strange to explain because sometimes I wanted the sex just as much, if not more than my partners. But a lot of the time I didn't, and I did not have the self-worth to say no.

Before my complete transition to sex addict I dated one woman who I still think of to this day. Ashley was an 18-year old girl who hung out in the same crowd as Lynette's friends. Ashley was dating a sweet butch woman, and they always looked so awkward together. Ashley, this beautiful, kind, sexy and caring woman with a bull dyke; go figure. Ashley looked like she should be on the arm of the quarterback of Tennessee State, not with a bull dyke. She had brown hair that landed just below her bra strap with hints of golden highlights, big brown eyes and a laugh that was catching. Her beauty intimidated most people, especially lesbians because they didn't know how to take a sincerely feminine beautiful woman. But her attraction to women was too strong for her to deny. She, like so many beautiful lesbians, was starting to believe that the only women who wanted her were bull dykes, and that was not where her attraction wanted to take her.

Ashley called me one afternoon and confessed her crush. She lived in Knoxville, a couple of hours from Nashville. She was a huge fan of Tori Amos and had purchased a ticket a while back when they went on sale in Nashville. She didn't have the money to purchase a motel and taxi to and from the concerts. I offered my house and myself as a taxi service.

The day she showed up she had a red spaghetti strap tank top on. Red on a woman is what we call in the sales field my "hot button". She was radiant and her nervousness about being in my presence was refreshing. We talked for a bit before I took her to the concert, and she opened up about being a virgin on all levels. Even though a lot of boys wanted to date her she just didn't have the same attraction for them as she did for women. Ashley had been raised in a Baptist family, and although she wasn't straight she still held herself in high regard and wanted to wait to have sex with someone special, a life partner. She struggled with her sexuality, as most beautiful lesbians do. When you catch the eye of so many men but you lean hard toward lesbianism it makes understanding your sexuality difficult.

Night came and I took her to the concert and dropped her off after all efforts trying to get me a ticket were exhausted. I drove around and listened to the music she left of this "Tori Amos." I liked it and understood Ashley's taste.

After an hour or so of driving around I parked and walked around the concert arena. I found myself in an alley reading posters on the side of the wall when a door opened up, illuminating a spiral staircase. I saw two big men and a woman with bright red hair walking down the staircase. The woman looked a bit like the woman on the cassette tape, but I wasn't sure. A limo pulled in quickly behind me and the redheaded woman locked on my eyes as she came down the staircase walking toward the limo. When she reached me she stopped, broke the stare and turned her head down to my feet and made her way to my eyes again. When she met my eyes for the second time she said, "green eyes" in the softest whisper. I was a bit perplexed but I said, "Yes, green eyes." She then turned to get into the limo and the two big men followed her. As soon as the door shut it re-opened and one the big guys peaked his head out and said, "Tori wants to know if you want to come back to the hotel." I didn't know what to do. I was starting to become an asshole, but I wasn't a total asshole yet. I hesitated and thought about Ashley; how was she going to get home? She would be so concerned, and that wouldn't be fair. I guess I hesitated too long, because then the decision was made for me when the man said, "Your loss." The door shut and people started running around the corner. The limo was gone. If I had left that night in the limo it would have been more respectful than what I was getting ready to do to Ashley.

It took me about 30 minutes to find Ashley, but when I did she was worth the hunt. On our ride back to my place I could see her chest rise and fall as she breathed. She was excited and her lips turned a darker shade; when a woman is turned on I've always noticed a swell or a slightly darker shade on her lips. I have made it a point to understand the female sex. If you know what to look for you know when you can and cannot seduce. I knew I could seduce Ashley that night. Seducing women is an art form, and I studied my craft intensely and often. Once we got inside I poured her a glass of red wine, and after about five minutes of conversation I started kissing her. Her breathing got deeper and her sighs got louder; as soon as the sighs were at the right level for her not to be able to say no I grabbed her hand and led her to my room.

I started to undress her to reveal a strapless red teddy. Her breasts more than filled the lingerie. Once my eyes locked on this sexy woman in the seductive attire I grabbed her shoulders to push her onto the bed and followed quickly to tear off the teddy to reveal her incredible body. Her olive skin danced off the candlelight and her nipples were hard and ready to be touched. What I did next was without any care or love. I wanted to hear her scream and I didn't take into consideration her virginity or the virtue she cherished. I found the center of her desire and I used my lessons given by Lynette. I brought her to climax within minutes. When her moans calmed she opened her eyes and her face and neck were flushed, as woman gets after climax. She reached out to me with her naked vulnerable body and wanted me to lie on her chest. I got up and turned to the restroom to clean up. When I returned she looked embarrassed, and I did not comfort her. I did not allow her to put me in the vulnerable position that climax makes every woman. I came out of the bathroom and walked past her and out the door to the living room. I turned on the television and waited for her to go to sleep. When she did, I got into the bed.

I spoke to Ashley once more to plan a trip to see her in Knoxville. Even though I was terrible to her on her first night of intimacy, she desperately wanted to have more of a connection to her first lover. She overlooked my lack of compassion and asked me to come out to Knoxville. I never showed up for the date, and I never spoke to her again. I think about Ashley from time to time and when her memory comes up it's not unusual for me to shed a few tears. I have spent hours on Facebook looking for Ashleys who would have graduated from schools in the Knoxville area at the same time she would have. But I've never found her. If I ever find her I would say, "I'm so sorry Ashley, what I did had nothing to do with you and your beautiful soul. I knew from experience that you could be someone I could fall in love with, and I just couldn't take another heartache. I'm so sorry sweetie; if I had the chance to do it again it would be very different. I would have made that trip to Knoxville with flowers and smiles and all the love I could give. I'm so sorry."

Once I had done this to Ashley it changed me, and I became a different person sexually. I no longer had the ability to make love. Although I have never found it, I began really chasing the "Lynette high". To this day, if I'm staring into space for too long Melissa will say, "Having a Lynette moment, Jules?" Sometimes she's right. I wonder if drug addicts have the same thoughts and they reminisce about their first awesome highs.

I began wandering clubs and zeroing on targets and plucking them off one by one. I could not get enough; I was insatiable. I would have the same conversation with myself as an addict would. "Jules, this is the last time." But a day or two would follow and I would be on the prowl again. Lesbians started to irritate me because they were hard to seduce. Women in general are less likely to give up sex to just anybody; they want a connection and the possibility for love in the future. It's the nature of a woman, lesbian or straight. My addiction wanted more, and the selection within the clubs was not what I was looking for. I wanted the high-class drugs: beautiful woman.

I started a new job waiting tables in a restaurant down town. There was a waitress who started to catch my eye. She had long blonde hair and stood 5'9. She looked like she belonged at Hooters or in a strip club as a featured act. I would not call her slutty looking, but pretty damn close; a man's fantasy, shall we say. When I didn't have tables I would talk to her, and she was receptive to our conversations. In time I discovered she was engaged to a Chinese American man. So I dropped the idea and just focused on the friendship. She was a fun girl and we had nice talks.

"Jules, I want to see a drag show. I've always wanted to. Will you take me?" Of course! Being the nice woman I am I told her I would take her. That Saturday night I picked her up at her apartment and we drove to the massive club down town. Once we had arrived we got our drinks and found our seats. Damn, I don't remember her name. That's terrible – when you have slept with so many people you don't remember names, only body parts. I'll call her Candy. She reminded me of a Candy... Holy shit, I think that was her name. It just came to me.

Candy wanted to sit in the front row so we found these seats right in from of the stage. After a couple of drinks the show started. It didn't take long for the drag queens to hone in on us. We looked like a couple and two attractive feminine woman together is a strange sight in a gay/lesbian club. One drag queen made her way off stage and kissed me on my cheek. She made us stand up. "Look, everyone: a beautiful lesbian couple. Wave to the crowd, girls." Everyone cheered and after that Candy started to lean in closer to me. What was she doing? She was engaged and in love. It didn't feel right, but whatever, I thought.

After the show we headed to the cowboy bar to see what that was about. I told Candy I was going to the bathroom and she nodded and said, "I'm going to do this line dance." When I came back I saw this really dyke-y woman holding her arms above Candy's shoulders and pinning her up against the wall. The dyke was taller than Candy and looked like she ate about 5000 more calories a day, if you get my drift. I went over to her and asked Candy if she was okay. She told me that she wanted to go home. I asked the dyke to please remove her arms, because Candy did not appreciate it. Let me be clear that this type of behavior is not something that I have ever experienced before or after this incident in a gay/lesbian bar. Women, lesbian or otherwise, are not usually physically mean. They can be cruel and if you piss a lesbian off she might key your car, but they usually don't physically threaten you. In the back of my mind I was thinking, "Jules, what in the hell are you going to do? You are 5'4, *Candy's* bigger than you! What are you going to do? Kiss the shit out of this huge lesbian?" Just when I was about to get my ass kicked a group of three women the same size as the super dyke came up and asked us if we were okay. Candy and I both put our hands on our hips and said no. These three wonderful women asked this bitch to remove her hands and to leave us alone. She did, and Candy hugged me like I saved her. Are you kidding, I thought.

We decided to leave and went to my car. Before I could start the engine Candy came to my side and started kissing me. I was confused. I enjoyed the gesture, but she was straight, right? On the ride home Candy was kissing me and revealed my breasts and started licking them. Strange, I thought. "Strange" was a word that would appear in my brain quite a few times for the remainder of the night.

When we got to her place she asked me to come inside. "What about your fiancé'?" I asked. She replied, "He's closing the restaurant and won't be home until about 4am." I looked at my watch; it was midnight. Candy's whole demeanor changed when I said I would come in. She became what I call a nasty woman. Nasty is something men enjoy, not women. Women like sensual, but Candy was all business. But I was up for the adventure and went along with it. I undressed her, sat her on the couch and spread her legs. I began pleasuring her. As soon as I did the door opened and there stood a beautiful Chinese American man. He looked confused. As I look back I think that Candy planned this and the man and I were just little pawns in her sexual game.

The man didn't say a word. He went to the bathroom and started to shower. Candy went in after him and their voices got loud. It was apparent that he did not like what he had walked in on. I didn't know what to do. I didn't want to be rude and leave. That's so funny; "I didn't want to be rude."

Candy came back out and asked if he could join us. I didn't really want him to, but I was excited and wanted Candy to finish what she had started. So I reluctantly said yes. He came out of the bathroom with just his shorts on and sat on the couch. He and I looked at each other and I said, "Hi." I started a conversation: "So you must be Candy's fiancé'?" "Yep, and you must be Jules the lesbian." Small talk is always the best way to overcome a difficult situation, don't you think? Before we could start another sentence Candy pushed me back on the couch and started ripping off my jeans. Sex with her felt like drowning; just when you came up for air you were taken back down. So much for small talk, I thought. Candy then took her attention to her fiancé´. She removed his shorts and started to give him head. My eyes widened. Holy shit, I thought, that's erotic to watch. Whoever said Chinese men are not well endowed did not include him in the evaluation, because he might have fucked the whole results to favor on the side of the Chinese men.

Candy grabbed my hand and pulled me to my knees. She removed herself from her fiancé´ and started to kiss me again. She started moving from me and I followed her, I didn't want to stop kissing her and once I opened my eyes we had this huge penis between us. She whispered, "Help me." Anyone who knows me knows I am a helper. If you need help, I'm there. Shall we say: I helped. "I want him to fuck you Jules, I want to watch." Then the strangest thing happened. This man grabbed my shoulders and lifted me from his erect penis like I was a rag doll and brought me to his face. I saw the most sincere, kind eyes and he said, "Are you okay with this?" This man was trying to make sure I was okay! I think he was searching himself as well. I told him I was, and with that he cradled me and took me to the floor. He was so gentle and kind, and he kept asking, "Are you okay?" I felt more of a connection with this man than with this crazy breast-licking woman. I think the excitement was too much for him, though, and he finished fast.

After that he got dressed and left the apartment. I was left with this sex maniac and I spent the next hour or so just trying to survive.

I left the apartment feeling used; I believe I felt the same as the man did. The next day I saw Candy at the restaurant, where she told me that she left her fiancé´. That poor man, I thought. The following weeks Candy and I spent time together and moved in together for a couple of weeks. She would bring men home and I was always jealous, but I knew that Candy was mostly straight and I tried not to expect too much. Candy was fun to be around and I thought I didn't deserve too much, so she was perfect. One night her fiancé´ came to the apartment and banged on the door, demanding that Candy come out. "Is that fucking dyke there, Candy? I will kill her!" So much for the nice guy, I thought. But I could understand, Candy was a total tease. Well, not really a tease, because she did deliver, but rather an emotional tease. The cops came and took him from the premises, and I never stayed another night with her.

The following months we still spent some time together and she introduced me to the swinging life style. She took me to these secret swinging clubs, and it was as if we were in some kind of movie. It was bizarre and ugly; it wasn't about an emotional connection. It was about sex. It was so long ago and I'm trying to remember the details, but all I can remember is that it seemed like we went to different rooms and you were paraded to see if couples were interested in us. Attractive women are a hot commodity, and two hot women made the ticket even hotter. The tricky thing is that if too much attention was paid to only the women, the men would get angry. When men are horny and angry it makes for a bad mixture, so a balance always had to be played. This was not for me and I stopped seeing Candy.

I called my dad in Miami and told him that I wanted to come home. He sent me money and I made my trip back to my dad's new house. I came up with this plan to be a salesperson; my granddad had always said that I would be a good salesperson, so I would give it a try. Why not? I was a terrible waitress. I went on a couple of interviews, but I didn't get anywhere. Then I landed a sales interview at Coca Cola. The job was traveling from grocery store to grocery store and selling the product. "Listen, aw, Jules...it's Jules, right? You need sales experience to sell; do you have any sales experience?" I told the man no, but I was a fast learner. He put the paper he was holding in his hands down and said, "Listen, most good salesmen are men, and you're not a man. Sorry, pretty."

"Sorry, pretty?" What in the hell did that mean? That didn't even make sense. I didn't even amount enough for him to say "ma'am?"

On the way home I had a brilliant idea: I was going to be a hairdresser. You're probably thinking, "What?" I know, me too. But I thought that if all good salespeople are men, and I wasn't a man, I'd do something that women did. I began school, but wasn't able to get away from my new addiction.

I started going to lesbian clubs, but lesbians are exhausting to seduce. I figured something out: mostly straight women are more feminine, more beautiful and easier to seduce. You would think it was the other way around, but it's not, and here's why: Mostly straight woman have these fantasies about sleeping with women, and their boyfriends and or husbands feed it. Couples talk and fantasize about bringing a woman home to sleep with all the time. Or shall I say, some couples talk about it all time.

To the ones that do bring it up over and over when they are getting ready for a night out on the town it's like foreplay. They go out on the town and they are meaning to have a good time, but this is always a thought in the back of their minds. When I would go to the clubs I would find the couple that looked like they were searching for something, but were never able to find it. I would watch and catch a glance and find my prey. I was never wrong. Sometimes it was a couple and sometimes it was just the woman, and I would make her dirty fantasy come to life in the bathroom of the club.

I would find myself talking inside my head telling me to stop, and I would try. I would say, "You are good enough to have someone like you and be around you without having sex with them." But I was awkward and unable to connect with people yet, and I would go back on the prowl.

In beauty school there was this woman named Denise. Denise was always sitting by me in class and have lunch with me. She was fun to be around. I could tell before she even opened up her mouth that she was attracted to me, but she never said anything outright, and I wasn't that attracted to her, so I didn't push the subject. Denise was married and I could see it coming a mile away, but I went along with the whole game. "Jules, I've always—" I interrupted her: "You've always wanted to go to a drag show, right?" "Yes! How did you know?" "Just a good guess. I can take you this Friday. Do you want to take your husband, or just us?" "Just us." I was so matter of fact.

Friday came. She opened her door and said really quickly to her husband, "See you when I get home, bye!" With that we were out the door and on our way to the club. I ordered a couple of drinks and we watched the show. After the show and a couple of drinks I got the, "I've always wanted to kiss a woman." I looked at her and said, "Really. What a shocker. Do you want to get out of here?" She said she did, and we made the drive home to her apartment. Here is where I made the mistake. Denise was not a mostly straight woman, but rather a mostly lesbian woman who didn't understand it yet. And her husband had no idea what was about to happen in his living room.

Her husband woke to strange noises and had the same reaction the Chinese American man did. I was irritated that they were taking so long talking in the bedroom, and I started to get up to leave. I was way past the not wanting to be rude. I was now at the "Let's get the fucking move on or I'm outa here people." However they both emerged from the bedroom and we went about the night. Once everyone was satisfied I left.

On Monday Denise was clingy and it made my stomach sick. I had become a one-stop shop. One ride, and that's it. I tried to ignore her as much as I could and I thought I was doing well until I got a phone call from her husband. He asked me to come over that night while Denise waited tables. He was almost crying and even though I acted like I didn't care, the fact is I did care and always have. Caring has always been my problem. But I never knew how to care for myself, so I couldn't care for others. I could not refuse his shaken voice and I found my way to his apartment at the time he requested.

"Jules, I'm leaving Denise and moving back to Oklahoma. I bought a ticket and I'm leaving after she goes to school tomorrow. Jules, she is in love with you, you are all she talks about. I'm giving her to you. Promise me you will take care of her." What? I thought. Wait a second, I'm not even that attracted to her! What is this guy thinking?

I didn't know what to say. I didn't know what to do; this man was devastated and I tried to reassure him that he was wrong. I wanted to comfort his broken heart, so I offered myself to him. That was all I knew how to do. He declined and asked me to hold him while he fell asleep, so I did. I grabbed his hand and took him to the bedroom and held him as he fell asleep crying. When I knew he was asleep I peeled myself from him and left.

I went to school the next morning and then went home with Denise after school as her husband had asked. He didn't want her to be alone when she found him and all his things gone from the apartment. The next two weeks were hell. Denise would cry and try to call her husband, but he could not be reached. He had made a decision, and it was not going to erased. She would try to get herself together and then wanted to have sex with me. I refused. I saw what all of this dirty, ugly, disgusting sex had done, and I didn't want it any more. That man changed me; he was a good man who loved his wife and just wanted to love her for the rest of his life. He probably wanted to have babies and watch them grow up. I never wanted to be the cause of any man or woman to be in the kind of pain that I saw in his eyes that night.

I tried to be there for Denise, but she started to get angry with me that I didn't want her in the way she wanted me, and we ended our friendship. I wonder what happened to Denise and that man? Did he get a wife who cherished him, and did Denise find a woman who cherished her? God, I hope so. I really hope so.

I finished beauty school and got a job cutting hair. My father blew up a month or so before I graduated, so I decided to move out and find my own place. Even though my dad had done everything for me when I'd had my nervous breakdown I didn't want to be on the receiving end of his rage any longer. Once again he "disowned" me. So I sold my car and used the money to buy a super cheap POS car. I put the rest of the money down on this dive on the really "bad" side of Miami. My apartment had bars on every door and window, and that gave me a bit of comfort. I just had to jump out of the car as soon as it stopped and run to the door, open the door and lock it before I got shot. It wasn't that bad, but it was a pretty damn close.

I had decided that I only wanted to date people I had the potential of having a true relationship with. Because I wasn't on the prowl I gained about 25 pounds. With my genes it was not hard to do. Staying thin for me meant not really eating much at all. If I wasn't trying to seduce women, I didn't have a reason to starve myself. I didn't inherit the big bones and tall side from my father, and being small it's really easy to gain weight.

One day I looked in the mirror and said, "What the fuck, tubby?" I went to the gay area often, where I saw a flyer for a gay/lesbian swim team. I thought it was time to try and meet people to be friends with, no matter how awkward it was for me. I was tired of just having sex. A swim team would help me lose the weight, and I'd try my hand and the friend thing.

I joined the swim team and lost the 25 pounds I had gained. On the team a woman named Spring caught my eye. Not because she was beautiful, but because she seemed normal and loving. She was cute in her own right; she had long blonde hair and a chubby but attractive physique. What she lacked in outer beauty she made up for in inner beauty. She was about 34 and was just finishing her doctorate degree in Psychology. I wanted to be her friend, and the only way I knew how to do this was to seduce her. She was hard to seduce and I wasn't used to this, so it frustrated me. However I wasn't frustrated too long, and I did get my way, as I usually do.

Spring's home was not something you would see in Better Homes and Gardens, but it was a home and it felt like a home. She wanted to see my place, so I took her one afternoon after swim practice. When we got to the area she quickly locked her car doors. "Jules, you live around here?" She looked all around and I followed her eyes. I was embarrassed, but told her I did. I unlocked the door and she stopped and said very firmly, "Jules, you are living with me. Grab your things." It wasn't hard to grab them; I just had clothes, no furniture. After I had all my clothes in her car we went to her house and she cleaned out a couple of drawers. "Here you go, sweetie."

I didn't understand what Spring already knew. We were not lovers; I think we had sex once or twice and I kept offering, but she never wanted it. She was like a mother to me. She started to teach me things, things that most should know at my age. How to act, what to say. She opened her arms to me as a mother and not as a lover. I was perplexed then, but I understand now. She would stay up for hours as I would tell her stories of my childhood, and when I would cry she would hold me.

Christmas came. We got a tree and she invited people over. I felt like I had a home. I began to sleep a lot, not because I was depressed, but because I felt safe and I was exhausted. She taught me how to cook a turkey in a paper bag, and that if you put double the oil in a brownie mix, it makes fabulous brownies. She encouraged me to join a lesbian soccer league and when I did she would come watch me.

Everyone thought we were a couple. She never corrected them, and she never corrected me either. I thought we were a couple, too, because why else would someone be this nice and kind to me? She wanted me to figure out on my own that the reason she was my friend was because I was good enough to deserve a friend.

While I was living with Spring my sister gave birth to my awesome niece Carla. She went through a horrible post-partum depression with psychosis. Jennifer had always hidden all of her tears inside, and when I found myself on the other end of the phone comforting her it felt strange. Spring would give me advice on what to say, and I would listen. Jennifer really scared me and the doctors finally put her on some medication that ended the psychosis. A year later she got off the medicine and has been fine ever since.

After a year or so, while I was getting ready for a soccer game, I turned to look at Spring and I said, "Spring, we are not girlfriends are we?" She replied, "No, sweetie." I said back to her, "You feel more like a mom." She nodded her head in agreement like she already knew this and was just waiting for me to figure it out on my own. "Honey, listen: let's just say I'm your lesbian mom. I didn't give birth to you, but I love you just the same." After that conversation I moved into the other bedroom. Spring was the first person in my life that didn't want anything from me but to give me love. With her Psychology degree she read me like a book and saw a wounded child that needed to just breathe for a while without worrying about catching rage or fulfilling sexual fantasies or allowing me to sell my body for love or friendship. She loved me and didn't want anything in return.

I grew up in the year that I lived with Spring. I couldn't count the hours she spent listening to me ask things like a teenager would ask a mother things. "Okay, so you don't have sex the first time you meet someone you are interested in?" or, "How do you know when someone is interested in you?" "How do you go about looking for a good job?" "How long does it take for a watermelon to go bad?" It's hard to explain, but when you have the type of childhood I had it stops your maturity level at the time the abuse starts. For me it was never-ending, so I would ask child-like questions up to young adult questions. Spring wasn't an alcoholic. She wasn't abusive; she was even all the time, and it was a blessing to me. It felt like I grew through my childhood years while living with her.

Let me kibosh any idea that the reason I'm gay has to do with needing a mother figure. Yes, I did need Spring's mothering, but needing that mothering had nothing to do with my sexuality. That would be the same as saying that having a terrible father makes a man gay. In my belief, sexuality is set in the genetics. What I have learned is that everyone needs friends AND a lover/partner. I was under the impression that to be my friend meant I needed to fuck you. "AS", as I like to call it, or "After Spring" I realized that I was good enough for someone to like me just because.

I moved in with Spring as a child and left feeling like I was an adult. What can I say; I'm a fast learner.

"Jules, come back to my office." I entered my manager's office and she said to me, and I will never forget, "Jules, you are a so-so hair stylist and I can tell you are not in love with it, but holy shit, you can sell product. Take a look at this." My manager rolled out this long sheet of paper that compared the averages of products sold in our region. I was way above everyone. I looked at the numbers and felt quite impressed. She said, "Have you ever thought about going into sales? I think you've missed your calling!"

I did want to be in sales, but I didn't think I could get a sales job without sales experience. Doing hair was okay, but she was right that I didn't love it. The reason I got into hair was to be around beautiful women. What can I say; I loved women. The way they smelled, looked, walked – just about everything. When I went down this road I was thinking that I could be around women all day and touch their hair, flirt and talk with them, and that this was going to be the best job ever. What happened was different than I had expected and probably had something to do with the triple-Ds. What I got was a huge clientele of men. They loved me. I would flirt with them, that didn't bother me. But I wasn't all gaga; men don't like gaga women. They don't. Sorry, mostly straight women! They like a challenge, and I'm the ultimate challenge. So from the time I came in the shop until I left at night it was, "Jules, Tom is here, Jules, Fred is here, Jules, Sam is here, Jules, Tony is here, Jules, Brian is here." Not what I had expected at all. When my manager pointed out my sales I was thinking that maybe she had something there.

With my past experience I knew that I couldn't get into sales if I didn't have experience. Or that was what I thought. The day my manager pulled me into her office I went and got a paper and yanked out the wanted ads. Right in the middle of the page there it was: "Salesperson wanted, no experience necessary." Awesome! I called and went in for an interview. It wasn't an interview, but rather someone telling me about an opportunity as an independent contractor. No hourly wage, no insurance, no nothing. In fact, I had to pay $350 for this opportunity. I only had $400 in my account, and rent was due in two weeks. I had moved out from Spring's house and had a little apartment she helped me pick out on the decent side of Miami. When the "interview", or opportunity meeting, was over I wrote my $350 check and got my supplies. I called my manager at the salon and told her that I was going to be a salesperson like she suggested.

I started selling for a company in the Miami area. It's a collection agency, and I sold collection packages that might or might not work collecting past due accounts for businesses. Regardless of the success I paid for the packages up front. Don't get me wrong; it's a great company, just an extremely hard product to sell. I went through my three days of training that I paid for, and once I was done I approached Steve, the owner/ manager for the office and asked, "Where are my customers?" He opened the door and said, "Out there."

I was so excited, but my excitement dwindled as my efforts produced no sales. Rent was coming up and I was getting really discouraged. It had been two weeks without any success. I was thinking about begging for my stylist job back. I went into Steve's office and went through a sob story. He listened and gave me some really good advice, but I couldn't hear it because I was doing a poor poor pitiful me.

Steve was well to do, you could tell with the quality of his office furniture and the Mercedes his wife drove to pick him up in every day. When the conversation was over he stood up to walk me to the door. When we reached the door he waited for me to open it and I thought that was odd. I opened the door and he walked in front of me. As he walked past me he said, "The one at the top of the mountain didn't fall there, Jules."

This a guy who had been selling at the company for a while said, "Do you know Steve is legally blind?" I said that I hadn't known that; he didn't seem like a blind man at all. "I bet he wasn't blind when he made all his sales ten years ago and was given this office." The guy said to me, "No Jules, he was blind then, too. He rode the bus to business parks and walked door to door and didn't let anyone tell him he was blind and couldn't be a salesperson." I stood by the door just staring for about 10 minutes. So how do you get to the top of the mountain, I thought? An image of a person came to my mind as I closed my eyes, and all I could see was a female image that was sweating from hard work and that has been my motto ever since. No one was ever going to tell me that I couldn't do anything ever again.

Something lit in my gut, the fire that had ignited the presence and voice that I found that day in Mexico when my mother was going to get raped and my sister and I saved her. My eyes fell in target and I was pissed, excited and ready to start this sales thing. I went back into the office and I asked Steve what he did to be so successful. I didn't take any paper with me to write down what he said, but I remembered it and logged it into memory. Every time he spoke to a customer I took a mental note on how he handled things. I bought a supply of door hangers, as he suggested. Instead of walking through the business parks and putting flyers on the doors I bought skates with my last check I got from the salon. That way I could do it faster. I didn't talk to anyone at the office unless it had to do with getting a sale. I created a mailing system with the percentage of commission I made on each sale. Weekends were spent canvassing for business parks and skating door to door.

As I started to be successful I saw my name go up on the sales board. Number one in the office; number one in the state; number one in the region. As I focused on sales my need to focus on sex or seducing women went down. I wasn't dealing with my addictive personality; I was just transitioning to a healthier alternative. The year was coming to an end, and I was on target to be the #1 rep in the southwestern division out of 360 representatives. I was jacked and so proud of myself.

But the more successful I became, the more pissed I got. The more voice and presence I gained the more pissed I got. The more things I bought the more pissed I got. I had taken so much for so long that when I seemed to be able to find my voice and presence all I was able to come up with was anger, frustration and rage.

The day of the awards ceremony came and I had just missed becoming number one. I know number two doesn't sound good, but I was still so proud of myself. As the last month had approached I sent a fax to a guy trailing me who had sold for this company for over ten years. It said, "Are you going to even try and beat me? This is too easy. I thought you were good." Apparently he didn't take kindly to the friendly note and turned it on in the last month. He called a whole bunch of customers, renewed accounts and beat my gross. You live and learn, I guess. Nevertheless I was proud. When I met the guy at the ceremony he told me that he "respected my balls," as he put it. He shook my hand and I smiled inside. I went from people in the sales field not even having enough respect to me to call me "ma'am" and rather calling me "pretty" to being respected for my inverted testicle or uterus. Pretty cool, I thought.

My father and I had started talking again and I asked him if he wanted to come to the ceremony with me as my date. When they called my name for me to give my speech my father stood up with me. He hugged me so tight and said, "I'm proud of you, little one." When I was giving my speech I could see his tears falling to the ground.

When it was over I drove my dad home in my brand new Nissan that I had gotten a couple days earlier. I took him to my apartment to show him the furniture that I had bought and showed off that my apartment actually looked like a home. When we walked in my father looked around. He sat on my brand new white couch, put one hand on each side of his face and started to cry. "Jules, you are doing what I could never do. I was never able to do what you are doing without the help of my family's money." I didn't know what to say. I went to the couch and gave him a big hug and said, "I know Pop, it's okay."

I started dating a woman named Karen. Karen was a tall, slender 36-year old woman. She raised money for the local gay and lesbian chapter in Miami. I decided that I didn't want to go back to my whore days, and that I wanted to find a life partner. Lord knows I had more women than 20 men combined; I didn't need any more sex. I didn't want that life any longer, and I had another avenue to keep my focus: sales.

As soon as I saw Karen I knew I wanted her. She had the same type of presence that Heidi had. These types of woman draw me for more than just sex.

Karen was hard to seduce. Fuck, I hated that. It pissed me off. I was 24 and she was leery of a younger woman. I wormed my way into her life and we talked on occasion. She asked me to housesit over a weekend and I left my perfume smell throughout her house. On her pillow, places that would remind her mind of me. The following weekend she had a couple of friends over and asked me to come as well. After several drinks she thought it would be a good idea if I stayed the night. I tried to seduce her that night and I failed. Lesbians – fuck, they are hard to seduce. Straight women are easy, but lesbians are hard. I left in the middle of the night due to total embarrassment.

The following day she called me and begged me to come over so we could talk. I said yes, but I was really embarrassed and would have been all right to never see her again. When I came in she handed me a margarita and we talked. She listed all the reasons why we should not start sleeping together. I was too young; she had just gotten out of a bad relationship; it would look bad in the gay and lesbian community if she dated a younger woman. Karen was like Heidi. She had a draw to her and people wanted to be around her. She was a leader, just as Heidi was. She was not necessarily a beautiful woman, but rather cute, with big blue eyes. After a couple of hours of talking we decided that it was best to just be friends.

As we were getting ready to say goodbye I excused myself to the restroom and unbuttoned my shirt to show off my breasts. Just a little, but enough to entice. It wasn't my intention to do anything other than to give her something to regret later in life when she thought of me. I returned to the couch and said, "It's probably time for me to leave. Thanks for the margaritas." Her eyes landed right where I wanted them to, and as I started to get up she grabbed me and pulled me back down. "Jules, I can't stand it. I've wanted you since the moment I saw you." Perfect, I thought, just want I wanted. My breasts were a great tool, and I took full advantage of them.

We dated for about a year, and we had great sex. Karen was adventurous and free, but she also knew how to make love. Karen was the first woman that I made love to after Debbie, and of course I fell for her. She was strong and would grab my arm and pull me to her, just as Heidi used to do. She reminded me a lot of Heidi and I missed Heidi, so she hit several hot buttons with me. Throughout the year Karen would tell me how she wasn't ready to be in a relationship, and in the beginning she dated other woman. After a couple of months I put my foot down and she agreed to a monogamous dating relationship. She never considered me a partner. She hid me from the community and I never understood that. I think they don't trust attractive women in the gay community, and we are not fully accepted. It's quite strange and I have never understood it. To this day I do not have lesbian friends; I think they are all afraid I will steal their girlfriends. If they only knew that their girlfriends were safe; it was the husbands and boyfriends that needed to be concerned. Anyway, I was a dirty little secret like I had usually been my entire life, so I was used to it. Plus, dating a half-committed woman doesn't make me have to deal with my fear of true intimacy.

Over time we started to grow apart because we were not growing as a couple. We had tons of sex and did just about everything you could do sexually, but emotionally she only let us go so far. A woman started to enter into Karen's life; a lawyer. Karen quit her job at the gay and lesbian center and was looking to go down a new road. This lawyer was looking for a business partner to start a practice. Karen introduced me as her "friend," as she always had. I was jealous at first when she started talking about her. But after I met her I felt safe; she was ugly and had no sex appeal. I was safe, I thought.

I thought wrong. "Jules, I love you and you are my best friend. I want to share this with you. I'm in love for the first time in my life." Great, I thought, so glad I could help you share this joyous occasion. I guess the fact that she had fucked me the night before was irrelevant, and I was to be uber-excited for her. I wasn't, and again I thought the only reason women came around me was to fuck. It was my talent and I was good at it, but I wasn't good at getting women to fall in love with me. With lust I was a black belt like Lynette, but love was not my forte. I came to believe that I was to be a dirty little secret, and that was my destiny.

Jules Alexander

Chapter 11
Melissa: My Biggest Angel

My sister had two children by this time and she was having trouble with her husband. After the Karen heartbreak I was in need of a change, so I moved closer to her. Jennifer had convinced her husband to move from Alaska to Spokane, Washington. Jennifer decided that she wanted to be around Jen during this hard time in her life. Remember? The "dude" friend. My sister is amazing to me; she holds onto these lifelong friendships and draws strength from them. Jen lived in Spokane with her husband and kids at the time.

I started a new career selling cars. I was good at selling for the company I was at, but the idea of starting over in a new city was too daunting for me. I found an ad for a car sales position. I got a job at a dealership that was perfect for me. The hours were outrageous, but they had a liner–closer system. All I had to do was find the people a car they liked, bring them inside and hand them off to a closer. These guys were amazing salespeople. Most people in the car business are really nice people that are trying to make a living like the rest of us, and that's what I found with the two closers at this dealership. How they took people from lookers to buyers was incredible. I have been in sales for over fifteen years and the best salespeople I have ever met have been in the car business.

My granddad used to tell me that I would be a great salesperson, and if I really wanted to learn about sales I needed to spend five years in the car business. Strange that he said that, and that's what came to fruition for me. I kept calling my granddad every month; even after he disowned me for being gay. If he answered he handed the phone to my grandmother. Over time he would say a couple words to me like, "Hi, here is your grandmother." I would talk to her for about three minutes and always say, "Tell granddad I love him."
"Jules, it's your mother. Your granddad had a terrible stroke and he's in the ICU. I thought you should know." I dropped the phone, ran to my car and made the ten-hour drive to the hospital. Once arrived I found out his room number and ran to find him. When I did I said, "Granddad it's me, Jules!" I was scared that he would kick me out, but I didn't care. I wanted him to know I was there. Of all the grandkids I was the only one that came to see him pass away. As soon as he heard me he tried to lift his head, but he couldn't. He started to wail and his body started to move up and down. I ran to his bed and said, "Ssshhh, Granddad, it's okay." He tried to say, "I'm sorry, Jules," but wasn't able to get it out. I had

never seen my granddad cry before. It affected me and I began to cry as well. "I know Granddad, I know you never stopped loving me." Just at this time a priest walked in and asked if he could give the last prayer for him. I told him no, my granddad didn't believe in God. He was a good man, but an atheist. I always tried to get him to believe. I have always had God in my life. But my granddad would never listen to me.

When the priest had left I looked at my granddad. He was shaking his head; he wanted the priest to come back. I ran down the hallway yelling, "Please, come back sir!" The priest came back and said prayers and did some other things. When he left I asked my granddad, "Do you accept Christ, Granddad?" He nodded his head yes. I said, "Then you have nothing to fear, Granddad. It's ok." Calm seemed to come over him and I lay down on the bed with him. He reached for my hand and fell asleep.

The next day my mom and I took him to his home. It was strange, being back with all the things that gave me such comfort as a child. I felt like I was home. My grandfather died in his home and he's in heaven now, where he should be.

This was starting to be a good time in my life. I had my sister just a couple of houses down; my mother moved from Alaska with her 4th husband and they opened up a little bar; I came to peace with my grandfather before he died and my Bipolar II was calm. Even with all these things in line I was still dealing with my lack of self-esteem. I wanted to have a partner, and I didn't want to grasp at glimpses of intimacy by giving myself up for sex. I wanted a relationship, a partner and a family. I realized the family-part was a bit of a stretch, but would settle for any companion.

The car business requires quite a few hours and the hours I had left over I was with my sister or at the local lesbian clubs, looking for that special one. The selection left little to be desired. Why in heaven's name do lesbians think that once they start carrying the lesbian torch it means they can trash the idea of being feminine or keeping their weight down is beyond me. I know I'm judging and grouping people into a box, and that is something that I don't like to do. But this has been something that I have thought about quite a bit. With all that said you can guess that I was disappointed.

A couple of times I did become frustrated and went back to my old ways, but it just wasn't the same. I had earned some self-respect. I wanted more and was starting to believe that I actually deserved better for myself. But when too much frustration came into play mixed in with hypomania I would find my old self rearing her head.

It was at this point that I became angry at God. I had always had God in my life. But when I gave myself time to understand my sexuality and gave myself the permission to want a partner I realized that this was against what most "Christians" believe. I wasn't able to understand that, at least in my opinion, religions place these boxes around people to make themselves feel superior to others. The "gay" thing is a perfect opportunity for the right-wing Christians to claim their superiority as "straight" people. What I understand now is that no one understands the true gravity of God, and trying to understand God is impossible. People use God for selfish reasons to justify behaviors all the time. Marriage is a perfect example. What a great way to keep a believer in a horrible situation! I have a friend who is in a marriage to a man who belittles and emotionally abuses her in more ways than I think she understands. Abuse has a way of seeming normal if it is given on a regular bases and over time. She stays in this marriage because she believes "God" sanctifies marriage as sacred, and a woman who leaves a marriage is a horrible, sinning person. But if you think about it, what a great little arrangement men came up with in the day! Marriage: "You belong to me in God's eyes, so you cannot leave and I can treat you as shitty as I want, HA HA." Bullshit. I would have to disagree that God wants any person to be abused and miserable in his/her name. But to say that relationships need to be nurtured and grown like a garden and when no more is being produced it might be time to move on seems a bit too uncontrollable.

So, the marriage thing was created in God's name. It is my opinion that marriage was created to allow men to feel in control of women. I'm not of the idea that it is not used in reverse with woman towards men who are deep believers as well. But I believe it was conceived for men in the beginning. What I believe now is that God wants us to be kind to each other, but not at the expense of losing ourselves. Keep your heart open to understanding the love and learning that is all around us.

My understanding and acceptance has taken a great deal of time and praying with God. But at the time I wrote God off as a bunch of bullshit and titled myself as an atheist.

At my dealership was a man named Bill Brown. Bill was a bit unkempt and didn't seem like the top-performing salesperson he was. In fact, when I first met him I thought he was probably a bad producer and not successful at all. Over time I realized that this man was an amazing salesperson; in fact, he is the most amazing salesperson I have met to date. Bill was a Christian, but didn't seem to fit the profile of most Christians that flaunted their Christianity. He drank, cursed and, I think, did a little cocaine from time to time. He was married to a woman and they had seven kids. Oh my God, that poor woman, I thought when I found out about all the children. I think I even said, "Bill, your poor wife's vagina." We became friends fast and I looked forward to talking with him during the times neither one of us had customers. I was starting to learn how to be friends with people. To most this might seem comical that I had to learn to be friends with people, but for me it was a hard lesson to learn.

Up until this time I really did or said anything to sell something. If I had to lie, I lied. Sales has always been like seduction to me, and I didn't hold myself to high standards and did whatever it took. In fact, sales is quite a bit like seducing a woman. If you don't have morals and love for yourself or the person, it becomes a nasty transition and it makes you feel terrible in the end. Bill caught onto this quickly and ever so gently guided me down the path of loving people into a car. If it wasn't meant to be it would be okay; another one would come along that you could love into a car. Strange, I know, and I'm not explaining it right, but that's what he was trying to teach me.

After a couple of months he asked me to have drinks with him and his wife after work. As soon as he said this my heart sank. I knew this would be like all the other encounters I have had with couples to date. I said yes, but in my heart I didn't want to go. I didn't want to lose my friend and all this respect I was building for him by being asked to have sex with him and his wife. I was not at the point in my life where I would have been able to say no; if asked I would have done it, even though I didn't want to.

The time came and I drove to the bar and grill and met both of them for drinks. We had a blast. His wife was so cool, and we talked and drank for hours. I knew though the time would come, and I just waited. The clocked ticked and I listened to every word carefully to get a hint of when it was going to come. "Hey Jules, it's getting late and we need to be at work in the morning. Are you okay to drive home or do I need to call you a cab?" I replied, "Ya sure, I can follow you." Bill was confused. "No, I asked if I can call you a cab, or are you okay to drive?" I looked into his blue eyes and then at his wife. I was confused, but grabbed onto the lead, "Yes, I'm okay to drive." We said our goodbyes. His wife hugged me, and so did Bill. I got into my car and smiled the whole way home. Sometimes you don't understand the positive effect you can have on a person by just being decent.

Over the months I became closer with Bill, and I went on and on about how there are no decent lesbians and I was never going to find a partner. I went into the search for a partner with such zest, but over time I became jaded. The gay scene is okay when you are younger and trying to get laid. But looking for a partner in this environment is not what I would recommend. The women either want to be men or do drugs, or are just trying to get laid, or... I could go on and on. I started down a poor, poor, pitiful me-path. "Bill, I'm never going to have what you have. I'm never going to have a partner or a family." He would just listen and from time to time say something like, "Jules, you will find the one God wants you to be with. Be patient." I would usually respond with, "Fuck God, Lord knows that's all he has ever done to me." He never said anything to me and never corrected me on how disrespectful that was to say. He just said, "I'm sorry, Jules."

I was giving up the quest for a partner and once again I was starting to go down the road of trying to seduce as many women as possible. One night I was in the local club and I had my sights set on a woman. I was making good progress. I needed a drink and headed up to the bar, singing along with "I'm too sexy for my shirt." I noticed a cute little blonde walking, or shall I say kind of swaying, to the bar. She had had a bit too much to drink and I could tell. I had noticed her when I walked in but I had already zeroed in on another woman earlier in the night. She walked right up to me and blurted out, "You are definitely too sexy for your shirt." I laughed and thanked her and went back to the woman I was talking to. About five minutes later the blonde came up to me again: "Do you want to go home with me?" I responded with the thank you, but no thank you, and with that she left me her number.

I didn't think much of it until the next week end when I came in to the club and saw her with a couple of friends. I had succeeded with the other woman the weekend before and thought it would be fun to go down this road. I sat next to her and we talked for a bit. I told her I was going to call it an evening. I handed her my number and said, "I don't call women, so if you want to go out give me a ring." With that I left. After I walked out her friend grabbed my number, wadded it up and threw it on the dance floor, saying, "If you ever call her I'm going to lose all the respect I have for you."

Two days later she called me. Her name was Melissa. Every chance I get I thank God for this amazing woman. Melissa has been touched by the angels of God and is one of the biggest blessings in my life. But of course I didn't understand that at the time, and I treated her horribly. I didn't realize the reason I treated her so terribly on our first couple of dates was because I didn't think I deserved someone so incredible. Strange, how your internal self-worth can mess with your mind and choices.

After a couple of dates I convinced Melissa that she was not my type, and this allowed us to become friends. We started hanging out together, eating pizza and playing video games at the clubs. We talked on the phone and started to learn about each other's lives. I had never really done this before. Usually I would have slept with her and then moved on.

My dealership was having an off-site sale for the upcoming weekend and we were busy moving all the cars to the off-site location. Most of the salespeople got their wives to come and help move the cars to the off-site. After dozens of shuttles back to the dealership to pick up a car and drive it to the off-site location we were successful in a record time of five hours. "Hey Jules, all of us are going out for some drinks after work. Why don't you come and invite that Melissa woman you are hanging out with?" I called Melissa and she met us at the restaurant. We were all bitching about having to move the cars back and how terrible it was and how we wished the dealership would hire people to do this type of dirty work. Melissa raised her hand a little and said, "I can help moving the cars back on Sunday, if you like." They were all excited about the idea of having an extra person to help. I on the other hand was so egotistical and thought the only reason she volunteered to help was to be around me.

Sunday came and I was sick with a fever of 101 degrees. I called Melissa to let her know she didn't have to help move the cars because I was sick. I was convinced that she would not want to go if I wasn't there. I hung up and went to bed to be woken up by Melissa around eight in the evening. She brought me some soup and wanted to make sure I was okay. When she knew I was okay she left.

The next morning Bill made a beeline for me. He placed his body in front of mine and seemed agitated. "What's up, Bill? Are you okay?" He pierced his lips and went off: "Jules, I have listened to your crap about being a lesbian and that you are never going to find a decent person as a partner. I have heard you say 'fuck God' over and over again and I said nothing, just listening to you. I thought you were telling the truth, because I never knew any gay people before and I felt sorry for you. My wife and I have prayed for you every night since we met asking God to find you a partner if it was his will. You are a self-absorbed asshole and you don't even see what's in front of you because I think you're so used to feeling sorry for yourself. Melissa came last night and helped us move cars for six hours. When I asked her why she said she came because she made a promise and that was the right thing to do. If I were single I would be all over that sexy little blonde. My wife even said, 'If I die, I want you to marry a woman like Melissa.' If I ever hear you start your bullshit about being 'gay' again I will punch you right in the fucking face." With that he turned and walked away.

I was caught off guard and I tried to rationalize my actions. But I knew he was right. What he didn't understand was that I didn't think I was worth Melissa. I worked for a couple of hours, but his words kept ringing in my ear. I couldn't get them out of my head.

I left early that night and went to Melissa's. We had sex, and as I held her afterwards I knew Bill was right, and I prayed I was worth her.

Melissa was raised in a religion that I call the hellfire-and-damnation kind. Her mother was over the top with Christ and praying and receiving every word in tongues from God. Strange, how her mother was married four times and had four children from four different men. I tried not to judge her, but I wasn't successful. I still have a hard time with this today. Melissa seemed to be her mother's mother and took care of her like a child. She would go to the store and buy her vitamins and other essentials an adult needs. Melissa was still involved in her church and was tormented about being gay. Her religion believes that living as a lesbian is living outside of what Christ wanted for her.

Before I came into Melissa's life she had had one relationship with a woman. After two years of living together the torment of her sexuality became too much to bear and she ended the relationship for "God." When she explained this to me it was heartbreaking; you could see it in her eyes. But along with heartbreak she gained so much love and stability from God. This was a head tilter to say the least, but it was and still is Melissa's struggle. If I set aside her struggle with her sexuality, her willingness to love God gave her a spiritual halo. If you look closely, you can see it surrounding her to this day. After a couple of years trying not to be "gay," Melissa wandered back into the lesbian club and found me.

Because Melissa and I were friends before we had sex it helped me get close to her quickly. I saw this amazing godly woman who tried to do the right things at all times. She prayed to help her make the right decisions that would help not hinder people. She had a forgiveness and calm that I had never seen before. But it started to happen. Whenever I find myself getting close to people I bolt. I mean, I bolt *fast.* That's why the sex addiction was perfect for me on so many levels. Sex = superficial connection and no commitment. Connecting with people hurts me; it actually feels like it hurts my insides. It is actual pain, physical pain. I don't know why; maybe it was my fear of abandonment that I felt, or actually not wanting the good feelings to end. Maybe it was the fact that I knew all good feelings usually led to bad feelings, and the bad feelings were exponentially worse than the good feelings. So I bolted before the good feelings stopped to be replaced by the bad. I don't know, but what I do know is that it is still extremely hard for me to trust and get close to people.

After a couple of weeks with Melissa on the new level made me want to keep this relationship intact. But, my head would start to cycle. "Jules, you don't really like Melissa. Don't you feel trapped? Holy shit, what are you doing, Jules? Don't bond with her! You know what happens! Superficial relationships are better; what are you doing? You are going to get hurt? Melissa is going to leave you; you're not good enough. You should just leave now. Plus, you don't really like her, right? If you just do something huge, like throw

Jules Alexander

a fit, break up or sleep with someone else I will stop tormenting you, Jules. Come on, Jules. Do something; fuck it up so you will feel better." I've always felt like the cycling is a demon. Not literally; I know it's not a demon, but this head spinning or cycling is a cruel punishment that no person should have to encounter. I couldn't stop it, and I didn't know how to control it yet. I still don't know how to control it totally to this day, but medicine and age seem to help.

One afternoon it was getting bad and so I flipped it the bird. The cycling, that is. I had the day off and Melissa was working. Since I stayed with her most nights she had given me a key. I couldn't stop the cycling, so I decided to go against the torment. Melissa had left her house at 7:30am. When she walked through the door from work at 5:14 she came into "our" house. I couldn't make the cycling stop, so I flipped it the bird. "Fuck you. I'm going to move all my shit in, then. You want me to run? So I'll get closer. Fuck you! I don't care if she's going to hurt me, or you won't stop torturing me with this constant cycling. I don't want to stop seeing Melissa." I spent the entire day moving my stuff into her house, gave my landlord the notice and rearranged her house for both of us to live in.

"Jules, what's going on?" Melissa was confused as to why all my stuff was in her house and why her entire home was rearranged. The great thing about bipolar II people is that we can do what most people take five days to do in eight hours. Once I'm tunneled it's amazing what I can accomplish. She handled it the same way she handles most things: with love. "So we are living together now?" I nodded. "Great! The rent is due; here's the envelope. That means I can give more money to the women's shelter. Things always work out for the best, don't you think?"

I didn't understand yet that my emotions were cyclical; they still are today, but much milder on medication. Number one, I didn't have the right medicine; number two, I didn't understand the cycle; and number three, I didn't have the benefit of age. The bad cycling outweighed the good by far in the beginning of our relationship. But I didn't let it win. I started to name this feeling "moving to Africa." Melissa knew if I said, "I feel like moving to Africa," it meant I wasn't feeling well. She didn't know what exactly that meant and neither did I at the time. But naming this terrible feeling gave it less power and it helped to just acknowledge to someone that I wasn't feeling well. When I wasn't feeling well I didn't allow myself to make any decisions. I would have these arguments in my head: "Jules, just leave, come on. You will feel better," to which I would reply, "Fuck you. I'm not leaving, I want to stay with Melissa." When I did this I started to realize that if I didn't react to these feelings they went away. Not reacting meant I wouldn't fuck up anything good in my life.

The good and the bad, right? The good is that I didn't react and I got to be with this wonderful woman. The bad is that I would have this anxiety sitting just under the surface at all times. Melissa gave me a sense of home, love, understanding and family. I was also at the stage in my life where I was making a decent living and tripled Melissa's income. The anger that I felt when I started making money in sales began to mount. I was no longer on survival mode. I wasn't trying to figure out how to pay my rent, where to find love, or try and find a place to fit in.

All the abuse and rage that I caught as I child wanted to come out, and it started to with Melissa.

In the beginning it was a gruff "fuck" under my breath. But the way I said it made her a little uneasy. She tried to soothe me, and because we were at the beginning of our relationship and the euphoria hadn't worn off, she was able to calm me down quickly.

Do you remember that dog that my father bought me as a teenager to help me come out of my shell? Well, that dog's name was Dusty. Dusty became my father's constant companion. They were like two peas in a pod, always together; always. My father built her a little place to sit on in his truck when they drove down the road. He decorated his house to comfort the tan Winnie dog. I wish YouTube had been out when Dusty was alive, because I think we would have had some priceless videos. My father would be drunk, chasing this damn dog around the house, and she would growl and snarl the entire time running from him. When he caught her he would talk in this little baby voice, "Come on Dusty girl, we need to brush your teeth, girl, you have stinky breath, girl." He would go on and on and it was like they had their own little language. In fact he would talk to her like this: "Dusty, if you need to go pee scratch once on the door, and if you have to go poop scratch twice on the door." I'll be damned if she didn't scratch twice and you could follow her with your eyes and she would find a place outside and take a shit. My father hocked a gold Rolex of his great-grandfather's one time to take Dusty to the veterinarian for some surgery she needed. My father had an intense nurturing side to him, and when Jennifer and I left he was lost. I understand he was abusive, but he had a very gentle side to him as well. Dusty made him feel needed and wanted, and it was a neat relationship to watch.

My father struggled with life, and his temper and instability made it impossible to have another relationship with a woman. My father raised Jennifer and I, drank and smoked pot. This was his entire existence; quite sad, really. After eleven years of life Dusty died. My father was a total wreck and had a bit of a nervous breakdown. He didn't want to be in Miami any longer, so he packed all his stuff up and moved in with my sister in Spokane, Washington. My sister was going through a divorce at this time, so it was a perfect match. It was nice to see my dad, and since I didn't live with him I was able to leave if I needed to.

"Dad? Dad, tell Melissa about the story when you were driving Jules's truck." One time, before I had met Melissa, I went to Miami and my father borrowed my little black Toyota Tacoma truck. I kept my vehicle immaculate, like my father did, but he told me he wanted to detail it while I was gone. I was no dummy; my father could shine a car better than anyone I'd ever seen. So he started: "One day, as I was driving around Spokane I noticed a lot of people being friendly and waving. I told Jennifer that Spokane people are so nice and friendly. Jennifer then asked me if the friendly people were all male. I thought about it and said, 'Yes, as a matter of fact they are male, Jennifer. Why?' Jennifer walked me around to the back of the truck and pointed out the gay flag that Jules had on her truck. I was so pissed and started to take the flag off for the rest of the time I was using it, but I stopped myself. I thought I'd just go with it. So from then on if a male pulled up beside me and waved I gave them a girly wave back and said, 'hello boys,' in the gayest voice I could come up with." This was the only time Melissa met my father. He told story after story and had Melissa rolling. When we got ready to leave my father handed us Tupperware filled with leftovers from the dinner he'd cooked. My father had come a long way from boiled chicken and was quite a cook. I still remember Melissa being so impressed with my father's nurturing. This was the only time Melissa met my father, and this three-hour visit is lodged deep within her brain. She is always telling me, "Jules, you and your dad have the same sense of humor." "Jules, tell me that story that your dad told me again. You know, the one where your grandmother knocked out your father's friend's mother. Such great stories, don't you think? Whose mother knocks out another mother nowadays! Things sure have changed."

One day I got a phone call from my sister. "Jules, can you go to Dad's motel? He's not feeling well and thinks he's having a heart attack." My father would go to a motel from my sister's house for a couple of days if he started to feel his anger get the better of him. "Jennifer, come on! Dad always thinks he's having a heart attack. Make him take a Zanex; he'll be fine. I've got to get to work." After a couple of exchanges I told her I would check on him. When I got the motel he was sweating and looked like he was, well, having a panic attack. "Dad, did you take a Zanex?" "I took three about ten minutes ago; I'm scared." I rolled my eyes and told him to call Jennifer if he needed anything else. "Dad, I have to get to work."

An hour later Jennifer called me on my cell. "Jules, I went and got Dad and brought him to my house. He doesn't look good. I called the ambulance." I rolled my eyes again. "Jennifer, why did you do that? Fuck, I'll turn around and be there in five minutes." When I got to Jennifer's house the ambulance had just pulled up. I went inside and saw my dad on the lazy boy chair sitting back. "Jules, come here," my dad said. "Jules, I love you, little one. I'm so sorry." I wiped his tears and backed away so the paramedics could work on my father. He died on the way to the hospital.

I remember driving home from the hospital and looking at everyone driving on the streets or doing their shopping, and I thought, "What in the hell is everyone doing? Don't they know my dad just died?" Apparently everyone else in the world had not gotten the message, and it was strange to see life continue.

Melissa did everything she could to comfort me, but I hurt. Being abused by someone is the weirdest thing to explain. Most abusive people are not abusive constantly. If you analyze the behavior of an abuser you can usually pinpoint when the blowup will happen. The abuse is the shortest period of time compared to the rest of the time you are with an abuser. If someone says, "I don't understand why women don't leave men who beat them or psychologically abuse them," I tell them that I do understand, "I totally get it." I was scared of my father for most of my life, but I loved him, and I missed him.

Shortly after this I decided to get a breast reduction. Melissa was not up for the idea, as she was "quite fond of them." But she didn't know all of my past, and looking back I believe I was trying to get rid of one of the powerful lures I had. After the surgery I became obsessed with the fact that I didn't want to cheat on Melissa. I had the cycling going on in my head about 60% of the time, and I wanted it to end. One of the ways I did this was by taking drastic measures to ensure I made the choices I wanted. "Melissa, let's move." My father had left my sister and I about $80,000 each, and I wanted to leave Spokane and just get away. Melissa wanted to go to ultrasound school and found a school in Tyler, Texas. "Great. Let's go." I convinced Jennifer to come with us, and we were gone.

Melissa and I bought a house in the middle of nowhere. Tyler was in the middle of nowhere and we were outside of Tyler, in the real middle of nowhere. Jennifer bought a house two houses down from us. My niece was five and my nephew was two and a half. This was a neat time for Melissa and I. I nestled myself as far away from any temptation and enjoyed my new life. My niece and nephew would run back and forth between the houses and Melissa would help the kids with homework while I made dinner. Remember the not-wanting-to-cheat-on- Melissa issue I had? I have never believed or condoned cheating on or with anyone; it's not right on any level. I know now that my conviction is enough, but back then I did not realize that I was strong enough without added help. So I went from being a hottie to 287 pounds in what seemed like the blink of an eye.

I was no longer the girl/woman that could catch the eye of most people she was interested in. I was not an attractive heavy woman. Melissa still loved me and wanted me in whatever form I came. That was worth so much to me. When Melissa and I first got together I puked up my past early in our relationship and then I would always step back. I wanted to bond with people, but bonding with someone as a child meant pain and abandonment. I am able to bond with people now, but it's hard and I have to really work at it. Bonding with someone takes a great deal of effort on the other side of me. I'm high maintenance now, but back then I was supersonic high maintenance. No matter what I threw at Melissa, she was still there, the same day after day. I cut off my boobs – she was there. I gained 140 pounds – she was still there. When I started throwing fits or temper tantrums, she was still there. When I would go on my ten thousand dollar shopping sprees, she was still there. When I called her 20 times until I got a hold of her because I was afraid she'd left me, she was still there. When I screamed about the house not being clean enough, she was still there. She was the first constant of my life; she never changed. She loved me, respected me, thought I was funny, felt cared for by me and trusted me.

Chapter 12
Kids

Melissa and I planned a trip to Seattle, Washington. We made a day trip to Tacoma, Washington. I wanted to show her my granddad's farm and where all of my fondest memories of childhood were. In the middle of our nature hike through what used to be my grandparents' farm she stopped me: "Jules, I want to have a baby." I turned and looked at her, confused. "What? Melissa, you said you didn't want to bring a child into a lesbian relationship." She shook her head. "I know I said that, but I feel like there is a child inside of me that wants to come out."

After the hike we went to my favorite Mexican restaurant in Tacoma and I listened to her talk about wanting a baby. She just lit up when she talked about it. I'd never seen her like this before. I knew at that moment in the restaurant that she was going to have a baby with me or without me, so I opted for her to have it with me.

Donor #457 was the choice after hours upon hours of looking at profile. We tried to match up the donor as much as we could to my physical characteristics. I quit my job at the dealership; I didn't want to work all those hours with a baby at home. I found a job selling cell phones in a mall. This new job was a blessing. After years in the car business, overcoming an objection on whether to buy a cell phone is like taking candy from a baby. I made more money doing this than I had done in the car business.

After two tries Melissa got pregnant, and I believe you could have seen the light illuminating from our bodies, we were so excited.

Seven weeks into the pregnancy Melissa began to spot. She went to the doctor and the doctor told her that she needed to just take it a little easy. What I heard was, "Melissa, you don't work, clean house, worry or lift a finger, except to make me food." I was two hundred and eighty seven pounds, ya know? So that's what I decided, and Melissa listened and took it as easy as she ever has in her life. Melissa had worked from the age of fifteen on to help support her sisters and mother. She didn't even get to go to high school because she had to supplement the income to help everyone survive. I didn't have to put my foot down too hard; she enjoyed the pampering. This is something that I gave to Melissa. I gave her the fact that she was good enough and did deserve nice things and to be pampered.

Almost nine months to the day Melissa woke up to go to the bathroom. Her water broke on our new carpet. I was a mess trying to just pick up the damn bag I already had packed. I finally got a hold of the slippery devil and made my way to the brand new Honda Odyssey. Hey, I didn't want the baby to come home in a used vehicle! I threw the bag in to find that Melissa was not behind me. I ran back into the house to a very calm Melissa on the phone with the doctor. "What is she saying?" Melissa pointed her finger at me. "Calm down Jules, I'm the one who's pregnant." I waited about thirty seconds. "What is she saying?" Another finger in my face. "Dammit Jules, call your sister so I can talk to this woman in peace." With her new wisdom my fat ass bolted out the door and down the street to my sister's house. Bang, bang. "Jennifer? Jennifer? Melissa's water broke, come on!" Jennifer opened the door. She smiled and said, "That's great! I'll get ready." "What?" I shouted, "Her water broke! I don't think that's good." Before I finished the word "good," my fat ass was running back to our house to check on Melissa. "Jules you dumbass, I told you to call her. You're 300 pounds, you can't run." "But I did, Melissa! I did just run, who cares, what did the doctor say? Do you want me to call the ambulance?" With that I bolted to the kitchen to get the phone. "Jules! Just take me to the hospital you idiot; she said it's fine. We just need to get to the hospital."

Then I ran from the kitchen to the van and the strangest thing happened. I couldn't find the driver's door, so for some unknown reason I began to run around the entire van, and on the second trip around trying to find the door I met my sister who had just driven up. She held her hand in front of my face, and it dropped me to the floor. "Get in the fucking car you freak! I'll drive." When I got in the back I noticed a very calm Melissa in the front seat, waiting for me to take her to the hospital. When she saw my sister she smiled and said, "Thanks, Jennifer."

On February 12th at 6:41am Kevin Alexander Riley was born. When the doctor gave him to me I had the best cry of my life. He peed on me. He loves that story, the peeing part. It was at that moment that I started to believe in God again. If you spend any time with me you will hear me say, "If you don't believe in God before you have a baby, you will believe in God afterwards." The doctor took him from me and I followed the nurse to the nursery. I watched them weigh him and change him. I told the nurse I would be back and walked outside the nursery, where I fell to my knees. "Thank you God. I will do my best, I promise." I then started to sob in a hallway of the hospital. "How am I going to do this? How am I going to be a mom? Please God, help me." After that prayer I had an ease about me. I knew I could do it. I have never felt anything like it before or after. I have prayed to God to help me over and over again, and this is the only time I felt like I was touched by God's hands. I lifted my head after that prayer, and my anxiety about being a parent was gone. I smiled and said, "Thank you, God."

Kevin was such a good baby. The only bad thing about him was that he did not sleep in a crib; he had to sleep right by me at all times. Not Melissa – me. We even tried to put him in the crib and let him cry himself to sleep. After an hour of crying we called the doctor and he said to let him cry, he will eventually go to sleep. We called the doctor back after two hours, and the doctor said that he would eventually go to sleep. At that point I said, "Fuck the doctor," and he has been sleeping with me ever since. He's almost eight now. It's not as cute now, but you reap what you sow, huh? Benefits of having two moms: moms are suckers.

About sixteen months after Kevin was born I was diagnosed with pre-diabetes because of my weight, and I looked into gastric bypass. I had not been heavy long; in fact it was a very short period of time compared to most heavy people. I got the surgery and started to lose weight quickly. I worried about cheating on Melissa, but she didn't let me worry for long. "Jules, I don't want to live as a lesbian any longer." You could have heard a pin drop. I was devastated. What I didn't realize was that my fit throwing or snide comments that cut her lack of self-esteem or my complete control I took over her and the money can be burdensome to any person. Mix in the fact that I was nice to look at about seven months of the entire relationship, it wasn't that hard to understand. I don't think Melissa knows how to leave anyone without interjecting "God" into the conversation. It makes her feel comfortable doing something that is uncomfortable. The fact is that I was hard to love and bond with, and she was exhausted.

We ended the conversation crying and leaving the ending open. It was as confusing as the last sentence was. I didn't know what that meant and not knowing what something meant or where it was going or what it's going to do in the future is uncomfortable. I don't like being uncomfortable.

It was at this time that I got a promotion into small business sales. My God, I believe I was made for this type of sales! Business sales, that is. I was an instant success. I broke many records and earned the highest awards within my company. I was noticed throughout the country, and these accolades were appreciated. I liked the attention, but I didn't know how to handle it. Within a year I was given a full relocation package to Kansas City, Missouri, as a major account manager. All of my colleagues had degrees; every single one had a Master's. I didn't even graduate from college, yet I had all these colleagues coming to my desk for me to help write business proposals for them. It was so simple to me. All they had to do was tell me a situation, and nine times out of ten I could find an open door. I would tailor their presentations for the door opening, and our team took off.

At home things weren't good, though. I didn't know if we were or were not together. All I knew was that Melissa was not working and stayed home with the baby, and I paid the bills. I thought we were together, but we didn't have sex and Melissa didn't seem happy. She wanted another baby while I was fine with one and didn't want another. I wanted to work on our relationship. This started to divide us even more. Because I felt threatened I would start to rage on the weekends and throw things at Melissa or demand the house be cleaner.

One afternoon I started looking for Heidi on the Internet. I had always felt like we never ended for the right reasons. We'd never had a chance, I would tell myself. I found her. She was in a committed relationship with a woman and they had a little girl, about eight months older than Kevin. We started to flirt via email and then on the phone.

Our draw was instant, like it always has been. I'm not good at cheating, and within two weeks of talking to Heidi Melissa found the emails. She called Heidi and they hit it off.

WHAT? I know, right? But they did. They really liked each other and still really like each other to this day. Melissa realized that we had unfinished business. She told me that she knew about Heidi and encouraged me to go visit her. Heidi and her partner of ten years were in the process of breaking up, so for some unknown reason I thought it would be a good idea.

I went to Nashville and Heidi was so much fun, like she always had been. She just soaks up life for all it's worth. She is a neat lady and we had fun for the week I was gone. But I missed Melissa and wanted Melissa, not Heidi. When I was on the taxi ride back to Kansas City Melissa called me and told me Kevin had broken his arm and she was taking him to the hospital. I didn't want to be away from my family. I wanted to be with my family and I decided to do everything I could to work out our relationship.

Over a year and a half Melissa tried to get pregnant every month without success. She went to specialists and they couldn't find out why; she just was not successful. We did not want to do IVF for our own personal reasons, so Melissa started to get depressed. "Kevin is going to have two moms and no siblings, I feel so sorry for him." When I got back from Nashville I told Melissa that I didn't want to be with Heidi and I finally had the closure that I so longed for. I wanted us to be a family and if she was willing I would do whatever it took to keep all of us together. I said I would even try to get pregnant with the donor's sperm. That way our kids could at least have the same father. Her eyes lit up. "You would do that?"

I realized this is not the best thing to do to try and save a relationship, but I'm so glad we did. The first time I tried I got pregnant, not with one baby but with two: twins. I always tell Melissa that she prayed so hard we got two babies instead of one.

My pregnancy was a double-edged sword. I felt great emotionally, but physically I was sick from six weeks until thirty-seven weeks. I would start the day the same way, in the shower sitting down crying and puking. I would dry my hair, heaving from the heat of the blow dryer. I would eat a couple of bites of eggs and puke on the way to work. After a couple of hours you would find me lying on the cold tile in the bathroom trying to get over the nausea right after lunch. The doctor actually put me on pills they give to cancer patients when they get chemotherapy so they can eat through the nausea. It didn't work for me, FYI.

After the second month I started to get these headaches that would not go away and that would make me vomit. Pregnancy was awful for me, and I often wondered why women would do it a second time.

My mother came to help take care of me in the last weeks of my pregnancy. My mother had divorced her fourth husband and whenever I needed her when I was in my 30s she always came running. She took care of me after my gastric bypass, with my pregnancy and after I broke my leg. Maturity gave her the ability to deal with her Bipolar better, but she has never gotten treatment for it. She does her best.

I woke up one morning in my 37th week with blurry vision and my mom took be to the hospital. In the weeks before I had been what you call a "Fly By Fruity" at the hospital. I had probably gone to the hospital no less than 20 times during my pregnancy. Each time it was the same thing: "Drink more water, you are not going into labor, you are not having contractions." After a couple of times when the nurses started speaking I would finish the sentence, grab the damn paper and say, "You guys are all fucked; I'm hurting." I became somewhat of a joke, and I started to play into it. "I know, I know. Drink more; I'm not having contractions. Give me the damn paper!" I would grab it and I was gone.

When I came in the morning of my 37th week I thought it was going to be the same thing. In fact, Melissa didn't even leave work to go with me. As I entered the circled area that housed all the rooms I said hi to all the nurses. I knew them by name at this time. "Hi Sally, Jennifer and Julie. How is Carrie's leg, is it healing okay?" I knew the nurse's names as well as some of details of their lives. My Nazi doctor came in – that's what I called her because she always said, "Jules, it's all just part of it," over and over again no matter what I told her. In fact, three weeks before this I had been in her office with Melissa and the nurse weighed me. I had gained sixteen pounds in five days. I told Melissa that this was it; she was going to take them. "Yep, Melissa, this is it. The twins are coming." When the doctor came in the room I waited anxiously for her to tell me I needed to go to the hospital. She came and looked at me and at some paperwork and said, "Okay Jules, see you in a couple of days." I replied, "What! I gained sixteen pounds! That can't be good." As she was leaving the room she said her famous, "Jules it's all just part of it." I had had it with the "all just part of it" shit. I followed her down the hall and into her next room where another poor pregnant woman was at and I began to yell: "At what point is it not all just part of it? For shit's sake, I gained sixteen pounds in less than a week! If I gained seventeen pounds you would you be saying 'Holy shit, that's it! That's the tipping point?' Or maybe eighteen pounds in a week? At what point is it not all just part of it, bitch?" The nurses entered the room where I was yelling at the doctor and tried to soothe me. Melissa grabbed my arm as I was crying in total discomfort. As I was exiting the poor pregnant woman's examining room I said, "See you in five days, bitch, maybe I'll have gained thirty pounds and you will shove your 'all just part of it' right up your Nazi ass!" I was a pleasant pregnant woman.

Towards the end I was done with the torcher. To say the least my doctor and I had a strained relationship. But she seemed used to it somehow; she was unfazed.

So when she came into the room and said, "Are you ready to meet your twins?" I said, "Don't mess with me, doc. Is it not just part of it now?" As she exited the room she said, "No, this is all just part of it too, Jules." I picked up a water glass next to my bed and threw it at her. I heard her giggle a little and I joined her. My mother called Melissa at work and told her that she needed to come to the hospital. She didn't believe her. I had become such a hypochondriac, or that's what they thought, that she refused to leave work until she talked to a nurse to confirm I was going in for a C-section.

Melissa held up each twin as they came out. I was so proud of what my body produced. Jason looked like a little lizard and Kelly looked like a porcelain doll. I loved my lizard and porcelain doll instantly. After the C-section they brought me to the recovery room, where I started to feel sick. After fifteen minutes I asked for some more pain medication and I was told that I didn't need it. I then screamed that I did need it, and a nice nurse came in and gave me a shot in my IV. When she was leaving she saw blood dripping from my bed. I had begun to hemorrhage badly. Apparently the pain that I was feeling for the last ten weeks was my uterus saying that it was done stretching. My babies were six and seven pounds, not the average weight of twins.

I called Melissa, who was on her way home to change, and asked her to come back. I had done something that was not within my personality type: I was completely organized with all the paperwork to give Melissa the authorization over me and the kids in case of an emergency. I had even come in eight weeks beforehand and gave copies to the maternity ward supervisor. I'm glad I did, because Melissa needed all that paperwork in a matter of minutes. When she arrived I asked her to call her mother. I was not fond of her mother, but I knew her church was connected to God in prayer. I didn't believe in God the same way, but I knew her church could reach God. I asked Melody to pray for me and I asked her to call her elders. I told her I had dreams of dying since I'd gotten pregnant, and I knew I had been right. "Please pray for me, Melody." As I was dozing out of consciousness I heard her say, "Jules, you won't die. You have too much help inside of you."

I woke up in ICU after having eight blood transfusions and an emergency hysterectomy. Melissa was there. Her face was drawn and scared. I instantly said, "It's okay, Melissa. I'm okay. How are the babies?" She started crying. I have seen Melissa cry twice in the fourteen years I've known her, and that was the second time. Ten days later I went home and two days later the twins came home as well. Kelly had developed a fever and they had put the twins in the NIC unit. Apparently the paperwork that I submitted came in handy for all of us. Melissa is quite a mama bear and had the NIC nurses caring for the twins the way she wanted. They had separated the twins in different beds and Melissa demanded that the twins be put in beds together. Once she did this Kelly started to get better. A mama knows, I say.

After I had the babies I thought we would go back to being lovers and a complete family. I was wrong. Melissa was still there and loved me, but in a different way than a lover. This time reminded me of the time I spent with Spring, although this time I was mature enough to understand what was going on. But I wasn't ready to talk about the elephant in the room.

If you are raised with consistency and love through your childhood, you start to sew what I call your comforting blanket. Each time your parents take you to a ball game and help you through a strike out or a failure, your blanket gets bigger. Once you leave home you have this wonderful comforting blanket that helps your through your trials and tribulations of adulthood. When I left home I had a one-inch square to the blanket, and I didn't have the ability to comfort myself. Melissa helped me build my comforting blanket. But this drained Melissa, and she lost her feelings for me as a lover. I had become a family member, a best friend and a co-parent. I was no longer a lover. After the twins were born my comforting blanket was completed, and I could see that Melissa wanted to be released. I asked her, "Melissa, do you want to be with me anymore?" She lowered her head and said, "Jules, I love you. But I'm not in love with you any longer." As soon as she finished this sentence she started to fall to the floor. I grabbed her before she fell to the ground and helped her into our bedroom. I laid her down on the bed and held her as she cried uncontrollably. "It's okay Melissa, let it out." I said something to Melissa that night which has helped us both through this time in our lives. This was what I call a "God" moment; the words that came out of my mouth were words I believe were directly from God for both of us that night. "Melissa, sometimes loving someone means loving them beyond what you need or want. It's time for me to do this for you." I held her for over two hours while she cried.

The next year we worked through this and realized that we are great friends and family but, as Melissa had already realized, we were not lovers. We didn't want our children in daycare, so I worked and Melissa stayed home and cared for our twins. We found that we were great roommates and friends, and we live together raising our children. In time this will change, but for now we have found a balance.

Melissa has embraced her church and has an even brighter glow about her. Now I feel as though I have begun building Melissa's comforting blanket with God. This comforting blanket is quite impressive.

Chapter 13
Today

My life has been a struggle in so many ways, but it also has been a blessing. I have fought through my childhood recluse issues, my fear of abandonment, self-esteem issues, Bipolar II, abuse, sex addiction, and my acceptance and love for God. I've gone from being a college dropout to the top business salesperson at whatever organization I've ever worked for. Because of all of this I think that I have been given the gift of feeling people. What I mean by this is that if I look at someone I can see the pain and joy they have encountered. I can see the anxiety someone is feeling, and I understand how to soothe it. That's one of the reasons I believe I'm such a good salesperson. I can feel what others are feeling, because nine times out of ten I've felt those same feelings. What a gift and a blessing to have the ability to have compassion for people.

If I hadn't been looking I would have missed so many angels in my life. Be careful what you say and how you say it, because you could change the entire direction of someone's life without even knowing it. The question is, do you want to hinder or inspire?

Judgment of another is just your own pain seeping out; remember that. No one knows the struggles of another or the heart of another. This is left for God to judge, because God is the only one that knows the true heart of people.

Bipolar II sucks, but it can get better. Abuse sucks, but you can heal from it. Addiction sucks, but you can kick it. You might not have self-esteem now, but you can get good self-esteem. You might not believe in God now, but you can believe in God in the future. Our life is ours to fulfill, and if you have suffered from all the things that I have, it doesn't give you an excuse to give up. You can do it, you really can. So if you are at the end of your rope and feeling helpless, just know to hold on to the bad long enough for the good to shine through. If you do this long enough, the good starts to outweigh the bad. It never goes away, but it can be so calm that you barely remember the bad anymore. I'm not quite there yet, but I'm a work in progress, like we all are.

Even though I write with such assurance, I still struggle. Please understand this. For example, this book has jolted anxiety throughout my body. Many times I have wanted to open my computer and delete it all. I gave a friend a rough copy of this book to try and see if I would be okay with publishing it, and because I think her husband is bipolar II and I thought the information would help her understand it. Man that put me into a tailspin. But I'm still here, and I feel a bit of a burden off my shoulders. Don't get me wrong: if I had to do it all over again I would not have sent it to this friend, because it made me feel vulnerable. I don't do well with vulnerable, and it makes me run like a little girl into the woods. But as I just said, I'm still here, and maybe it was the right thing to do. Maybe it's time to release all this stuff. Maybe?

I keep going back and forth with all this anxiety and I've decided that it's time to go to therapy. I've never been to therapy for healing, just for survival. I've only gone when I was in a complete anxiety tailspin. Now, with the right medicine, maybe it's time to go to heal from all this abuse. I have this image of what the first therapy session is going to be like: "So, Jules, tell me about your childhood." I casually open my bag and pull out this book. I place it on my new therapist's lap and say, "Study this for our next week's session." I then walk out, saying, "Let's get this shit on the road next week though, doc!"

So, to end my book I wanted to share a story on how it began. So if this book has helped you say out loud, "Thank you, Sofia." Oh Sofia, my beautiful Italian muse. A sincere Thank you.

Remember the job I got after I lost my big time job? The story starts as I walked into the first morning meeting at my new company. I looked up to see the most beautiful woman I have ever seen. I shook my head to see if my eyes were playing tricks on me. In the process I almost fell off my chair. "Hold it together, Jules." Then a thought entered my mind: "If God gave me the ability to put together the physically perfect woman, she would look like this woman." She used reading glasses in the meeting, and I was surprised because she didn't look old enough to use them. It turned out that she was 48.

In my opinion, women don't start coming into their age until they are in their 40s or 50s, so it didn't surprise me. Beauty needs time to mature.

I told myself to avoid her at all cost. I couldn't, because when I sell an account I have to get approval from her on one portion of the paperwork. Each time I did this, I asked a little question, for example: "What nationality are you?" Italian; how interesting, I say to myself. She reminded me of Sofia, and I found it interesting that she was the same nationality and age of Sofia. Over time we talked for sometimes up to an hour in her office. It turned out that this woman was nothing like Sofia emotionally though; she might look like a bit like Sofia, but she had the God-loving heart of Melissa. She was interesting, smart, engaging and incredibly sexy. So what should I do, given that she is a married and a mostly straight woman? I started avoiding her as much as I possibly could.

After a year at this company I had successfully and ever so subtly avoided her because of the obvious reasons. So when it was announced that she was going to take on a sales team I thought, "Please God, don't let me get on her team. I will be a love-struck puppy in a matter of days." I also knew that there was no way my manager was going to give me up without a fight, so I relaxed. Until I got the call: "Jules it's Don, listen: I've been dreading to have to tell you this, but you have been transferred to Sofia's team." Now, my manager was a "Jesus freak" and I tried to keep my cursing down to a minimum. I could tell it made him uncomfortable. But about five seconds after he told me the news I laid into a machine gun's worth of curse words. "Holy fucking shit, Don, no! It can't be! Please, change me back. Seriously, this is bad, man, really fucking bad. Shit, I'll talk to the director! He can change me back, right? Oh, fuck, no! Not her, Don! Come on, really? Why, God, WHY are you testing me? Fuck, fuck, fuck! Don, God dammit change me back, just change me back!" Don scratched his head and took it as a compliment. I'm glad he did, because he was a great manager.

Over the weekend I followed Melissa around going on and on about working with Sofia and she said, "Calm down, Jules. Tons of men work with women they have crushes on." With her newfound wisdom I wrote an email to Sofia and asked her, "what stars aligned for you to get me on your team," along with some other things about how great it had been working with Don. I think she could tell that I didn't want to leave Don's team. She didn't know why, but she could get the drift from the subtle but nice email.

Don called her that Monday and asked to keep me on his team. She says she doesn't know why she said yes to Don. Usually she would have said, "No way, Jules is the best salesperson I got, and I'm keeping her." But she let me go back to Don's team.

Okay, so now I was pissed, right? I was thinking that I was going to be able to smell her intoxicating perfume and have a reason to talk with her several times a day. I wasn't thinking right, I know. So I wrote her an ever so clever email back, asking, "Why is it that you guys are bouncing me back and forth like volleyball? I thought I was a good salesperson."

Her email back, word for word:

"Jules have you ever thought about writing? You are such a funny writer!"

The following night:

Chapter 1
Understanding the Beginning.

Jules Alexander

Sex Is For Love

Jules Alexander

www.ingramcontent.com/pod-product-compliance
Lightning Source LLC
Chambersburg PA
CBHW031211270326
41931CB00006B/509